100

THINGS TO DO IN
PORTLAND
MAINE
BEFORE YOU
DIE

100

2nd Edition

THINGS TO DO IN
PORTLAND
MAINE
BEFORE YOU
DIE

• •

ROBERT WITKOWSKI

REEDY PRESS

Library of Congress Control Number: 2018940104

ISBN: 9781681061603

Design by Jill Halpin

Printed in the United States of America
18 19 20 21 22 5 4 3 2 1

Please note that websites, phone numbers, addresses, and company names are subject to change or cancellation. We did our best to relay the most accurate information available, but due to circumstances beyond our control, please do not hold us liable for misinformation. When exploring new destinations, please do your homework before you go.

Back cover image: Courtesy of Samantha Witkowski

DEDICATION

For my aunt Karen Stephens.

Your encouragement, unconditional love, and support has given
me courage to fearlessly pursue a creative life.
I owe you so much more than these words.

And for my daughters, Samantha and Alexandra.

It is not an accident you grew up in this wonderful city.
Having Portland as your benchmark makes it all the more fun to
watch you discover the cities that suit your styles!

CONTENTS

• •

Music and Entertainment

• •

Sports and Recreation

• •

Culture and History

● ●

Shopping and Fashion

PREFACE

It is no accident I live in Portland, Maine. Portland is not for everyone. It's not enough that you want to be here. Portland has to want you to be here, too. The longer I stay, the more the people of Maine open up, and the more I learn about this wonderfully captivating and exciting city!

When approached to select one hundred life-worthy things to do in Portland, I thought it would be easy to compile. I quickly realized I was wrong. My preliminary list was way more than one hundred. Cuts needed to be made.

These 100 Things selected are not related to my my role in Visit Portland. They were chosen based on my personal criteria derrived from my experienecs in Portland over the past decade. Each of the final 100 Things to Do was selected based on its own merit, within the following criteria (which still required cutting!):

- Within Portland city limits (there are a few exceptions, but they snuck in by having Portland-based transportation and extraordinary iconic relevance to Portland)

- Uniqueness and/or significance in the city

- Something the general public can do ("Things" in private organizations listed are still accessible—events in exclusive clubs, however cool, are not included)

- Things I personally experienced as a participant or spectator. For the few I have not, I extensively interviewed those who could convey its worthiness and bring what makes it exciting to you effectively and accurately

- I attempted to avoid duplication, so while there may be many extraordinary places that do similar things, I single out those

I determined to be the worthy of the list. For any that seem repetetive, there are distinctive features that separate them from the others

- Items selected needed to be well established or, if recently established, demonstrate staying power with a commitment from organizers for a reliable future

The end result surprised even me. I was struck by the cross section of the final 100.

As in most cities, things change, places close, and (as the title indicates) people die. Apologies in advance if anything in this list is unexpectedly altered, or in some way inaccurate, dated, misspelled, or just plain wrong, I beg forgiveness. I have made every effort to get it right, but research can be flawed, people have revisionist history, and information may be misinterpreted. If that occurs, I apologize.

Please know that if you are on this list, or quoted in it, the reason is because I believe you to be one of the best friggin' things to do in Portland! I cannot possibly mean insult or harm because I truly believe you're offering something fulfilling in life—go with that!

The other side of that coin is that just because you aren't on the list doesn't mean you aren't awesome, too! Maybe you're just #101. I am aware I may get berated by several friends and associates who may demand to know why they didn't make the book. It's just that I needed to stop at one hundred.

Portland and the surrounding metropolitan region is one of the greatest urban areas to live in this country. Why else would I choose this seaside landscape as my home after living in Chicago, Boston, and New York City? Portland offers much of what is enjoyable about larger cities with almost none of the aggravations.

If I can't show you this city in person, I am honored to be here with you in words. Please enjoy.

• •

ACKNOWLEDGMENTS

To all the people in my life who supported me in so many ways, whether they knew it or not, in writing this book. It is because of their encouragement, enticements, goading, and simply inviting me to join them in escapades around Portland that I am able to present these one hundred things worthy of the last minutes of life. Their love and friendship were critical (literally and figuratively) in my writing this book.

Thanks to Bill Ryan and Grete Zemans for their time, patience and honesty in reading—and re-reading *100 Things to Do in Portland Before You Die*. Their efforts reading this when it was unreadable will (hopefully) spare me great embarrassment and ensure a (hopefully) fun and informative read.

Deep appreciation for my daughters, Samantha and Alexandra, for suffering through my nights out researching (see, it wasn't all just a lot of fun!), the days out writing, alleviating my concerns, enduring repeated readings out loud, and telling me how great it is with patient eye rolls and forgiving smiles. Gratitude for Craig Barnes and Chris Riccardo who forced me to go out and relax, even though they didn't always know why.

I also thank all the people who trusted me enough to let me in and take the time to speak with me, quoted in the featured 'things.' Hope I did you all proud!

Special gratitude to Ed Suslovic. I am humbled by his taking valuable time from his schedule to offer a forward to this book. His dedication and love for Portland is evident in his contribution, and I'm proud to have his words and friendship.

I am deeply appreciative of the jobs and associates who've welcomed me, friends who've made me family, and the city that fits me so well.

● ●

FOREWORD

Portland, Maine, and Robert Witkowski—a perfect match!

Let's start with Portland. A city with a big heart, an even bigger appetite, and a presence that burrows deeper and deeper into your heart the longer you live here. Comfortable, casual, yet with the ability to surprise you when you least expect it. Creative energy pulsing through the veins of her people resulting in colorful bursts of innovation which attracts more creative types and . . . well, you get the picture.

Now we come to Robert "Bob" Witkowski. See above. No, really! Bob is the personification of all the best attributes of Longfellow's "City by the Sea." Not only has he become part of Portland's vibe, but is a major contributor to the vibrancy which has placed Portland on just about every Top Ten list around. Going out to lunch with him means good food, great company, and making new acquaintances leaving you pleasantly sated gastronomically and socially. Boring is never a word used to describe Bob as he and his family excel at creating adventure and excitement wherever they explore. I get to live vicariously through Bob. Anytime I start to think that I know all that Portland has to offer, Bob sneaks one past me, and I'm following his lead on another fascinating adventure.

I know that every reader will want to join me in thanking Bob for showing us parts of Portland unknown to us until now. It takes a curious creativity to ferret out the individual strands of DNA that come together and create this city that never lets us down. Enjoy!

Edward J. Suslovic

—*Maine House of Representatives, District 32, 2002-2004*
—*Mayor of Portland, 2007-2008*
—*Portland City Councilor, 2005-2008, 2010-2014*

• •

FOOD AND DRINK

TOAST THE TOWN
FROM TOP OF THE EAST

Top of the East is the only rooftop bar and gastropub in the city with commanding views of the Portland skyline and harbor. Located at the Westin Portland Harborview Hotel in the Arts District, the cocktail lounge's name is derived from its perch atop the 1927 high-rise originally named the Eastland Park Hotel.

Listed on the National Register of Historic Places, this iconic downtown hotel has famously hosted celebrities from Charles Lindbergh to Julia Roberts—but not First Lady Eleanor Roosevelt... she was refused because of her dogs. ("Dogs are now welcomed by the Westin brand," winks general manager Bruce Wennerstrom.)

A recent $50 million hotel renovation doubled Top of the East's size. Stunning views of water, woods, and New Hamphire's White Mountains surrounding the Forest City afford a 360-degree panorama. Sunsets give way to the glow of city lights and flashes of the harbor lighthouses. A Dark and Stormy cocktail, anyone?

157 High St., 207-517-8818
westinportlandharborview.com/top-of-the-east

GRILLED MUFFIN
AT BECKY'S DINER

There's something about the blueberry muffins toasted on the grill at Becky's Diner that transcends all other muffins. A portside eatery for early-rising fishermen, many nine-to-five suits, and late-night truckers, Becky Rand's "long-running, no-nonsense diner" on Hobson's Wharf has been serving Portland's working waterfront since 1991 with "homemade food for a fair price coming out of our kitchen." Guy Fieri dropped in for an episode of Food Network's *Diners, Drive-Ins, and Dives*. Not to be outdone, Taylor Swift had an after-hours supper with her cast and crew after a long day filming her music video for her song "Mine."

Keeping its reliable commitment of a warm meal waiting for the erratic schedule of the fishing industry, Becky's remains open 362 and a half days a year, 4 a.m. to 10 p.m., only closing on Thanksgiving, Christmas Eve night, and Christmas Day.

Make sure to grab a souvenir of your visit: a bumper sticker telling the world, "Becky's Diner—Nuthin' finah."

390 Commercial St., 207-773-7070
beckysdiner.com

TIP
Don't mind the line out the door—they're just landlubbers waiting for a table. Excuse yourself past the snarling flatlanders and find an open stool at the counter for immediate service.

DINE DOCKSIDE
AT DIMILLO'S ON THE WATER

Feast on chowder, fish, and lobster presented in traditional or playful ways, including DiMillo's lobster mac & cheese and deep-fried lobster tails, while soaking in the sea air on this carferry-turned-floating-restaurant docked on the waterfront.

This Old Port institution was dangerously close to being a tourist trap when the second generation of the DiMillo family revamped their namesake restaurant. The most notable change was piping aboard Chef Melissa Bouchard. Her impact is tasted in a culinary approach focusing on accentuating Maine's agriculture and seafood with simply prepared cuisine.

Tony's son, Johnny DiMillo, emphasizes the restaurant's upscale but unpretentious appeal by saying, "We don't cook complicated masterpieces, just good food from fresh ingredients."

In 1982 Tony DiMillo opened New England's only coastal floating restaurant in what had been a seedy red light district in the 1970s. Many regard this as a turning point in Portland's waterfront renaissance. An instant hit when it opened, foodies craving the seaport experience thrill at the innovative renovations that make the ship a fine dining experience. Now, Tony's children and grandchildren literally keep the business afloat.

25 Long Wharf, 207-772-2216
dimillos.com/restaurant

Commissioned the *New York* in 1941 as a car ferry, the vessel serviced automobiles crossing the Delaware River, James River (as the *Norfolk*), and Narragansett Bay (as the *Newport*). Tony DiMillo had the hulk redesigned, making the car bay a spacious dining room with cocktail lounge. A portside deck was added later.

• •

Parking is easy on Long Wharf. If you park to shop, plan a quick bite before you leave . . . it's completely free if you validate your parking ticket after eating at DiMillo's on the Water.

ENJOY A FIRST SUPPER
AT GRACE

Entering Grace Restaurant, hosts greet patrons at a wooden pulpit in the former Chestnut Street United Methodist Church. Guests can opt to enjoy an aperitif in the choir loft above or a drink at the eternal-ring bar in the transept while waiting for a table. Up to one hundred diners bask in the glow of a massive rose window imported from Florence in the mid-1800s. Their meals are expertly crafted in an open kitchen where the altar once stood, appropriately making meals including lamb and fish for supper.

The Gothic church building (ca. 1856-57) next to city hall is one of the only surviving examples of architect Charles Alexander. On the National Register of Historic Places as an example of early Gothic Revival style in Portland, it's also one of the few structures to survive the Great Fire of 1866 that destroyed two-thirds of the city.

Architect Dean Bingham (who also sidelines as confectionaire extraordinaire owner of Dean's Sweets) presents an innovative vision in this adaptive-reuse wildly popular among foodies since the restaurant's 2009 opening. This unique preservation alone is deserving of gastronomic genuflection.

The reimagined choir-loft bar is a prefect perch for celebrity sightings, as nationally renowned talent often unwinds with a post-performance bevy, bite, or party after a show at the adjacent Merrill Auditorium or another nearby concert hall.

15 Chestnut St., 207-828-4422
restaurantgrace.com

SHUCK IT UP
AT J'S OYSTER HOUSE

Taking the cobblestone way past the docked lobster boats behind Commercial Street's curved Thomas Block building, is J's Oyster, a local institution where the regulars will never let you feel like a stranger. The waterfront eatery anchors Long Wharf. Its size is not deceptive—a U-shaped oyster bar fills the single-room, leaving little room for the crowd making its way around the joint, being further squeezed by a few tables against the walls.

Don't go for the view. Most seats at J's face inward, and the people come for the bivalve mollusks and the generous pours. Oysters are best in cold water, so rule of thumb is to eat them in months that have an 'R'—September through April. Occasionally stopping in for a nightcap, locals work May through August when J's is invaded by tourists who sit wharf side enjoying Chesapeake Bay-harvested oysters,

Working waterfront nighthawks mix with nearby office sharks to fill J's most any night—kind of a seafood Cheers. Walking into the bar can seem intimidating, but by the second round, welcoming banter from any of J's bartenders or expert shuckers will morph into customer cross-talk. Before another round, visitors feel like family.

5 Portland Pier, 207-772-4828
jsoysterportland.com

GET FREE ICE CREAM
AT SUSAN'S FISH-n-CHIPS

Greater Portland families descend on Susan's Fish-n-Chips four times a year when Susan's motivates area school children with free ice cream for good report cards.

Cards must be the most recent marking period up to grade six, and they need to have them reviewed by staff. Kids delight as employees heap accolades on students' accomplishments—some students seem to enjoy that more than the ice cream! There is no purchase needed for children to be awarded their cup or cone; however, the restaurant offers an obvious solution for dinner while collecting your student's tasty reward.

Formerly a Morrills Corner auto repair shop on a busy road, Susan Eklund's family-run restaurant is not what most expect when imagining a quaint seafood shack in Maine. Looks are deceiving though. Once inside, the decor is decked with ship wheels, lobster traps, and fishing nets, and the back patio makes diners forget they're not at the shore. Live lobsters troll their tanks and fish fresh off the boat are on the menu. Reasonably priced with alternative choices for carnivores and vegetarians, it's a local favorite no matter the GPA.

1135 Forest Ave., 207-878-3240
susansfishnchips.com

WALK INTO OZ
AT SILLY'S

Patrons crowd Silly's two 1909 buildings, eager for the extensive—and largely vegetarian and vegan—menu that appeals to all appetites. Locals know to spill into the hidden garden in back. "It's like walking into Oz!" says regular patron Chris Riccardo.

Large and lush, the outdoor patio makes city dwellers "forget where they are." Crushed stones and shells line paths snaking through foliage with tables throughout. A "humongous two-tiered deck with vibrant colors" looms from the connected Silly's With a Twist as an unexpected complement. The sudden remoteness and the lofty perch offers intoxicating sunsets away from the world.

Silly's understated storefronts belie its gastronomic oasis in the city's culinary scene in both atmosphere and heart health—even when not always obvious. "It's a salad with an explosion coming out of a glass . . . with strips of bacon," Riccardo says of the pioneering eatery's popular Bloody Mary cocktail.

Bordering the East End and East Bayside neighborhoods, Silly's opening in 1988 was way ahead of it time. When it moved to the current location in 1997, it remained the only restaurant on the now-popular Washington Avenue corridor for close to a decade. It's now a stoic anchoring a burgeoning neighborhood undergoing a rapid gentrication.

40 Washington Ave., 207-772-0360
sillys.com

SOAK IN THE CITY
AT WOODFORD F&B

"I don't think it is exaggerated to say that the building is what started this whole thing," Woodford Food & Beverage owner Birch Shambaugh told Greater Portland Landmarks of the restaurant's Mid-Century Modern curved-glass facade.

Formerly the flagship of the Portland-based Valle Steak House's twenty-five restaurants, the vaulted roofline was designed to emulate the popular chain's crown logo, unfolding like a hand fan on the west side of Woordfords Corner. The location looks directly at Odd Fellows Hall, whose eighty-foot-tall clock tower presides over the intersection, with a sightline down Forest Avenue to the downtown skyline Edward Hopper would envy.

On the edge of an exciting transformation, the five-corner intersection is a central hub in the city off-peninsula, with Woodford F&B introducing a cosmopolitan element missing from the trendy bakeries, ethnic markets, and diners sprinkled among the surrounding streets.

And ever respectful of the building's past, co-owner Fayth Preyer was excited to restore the original terrazzo floors.

660 Forest Ave., 207-200-8503
woodfordfb.com

VINTAGE WINE
ON A VINTAGE VESSEL

Sommelier Erica Archer leads wine wannabes on an educational Wine Wise tasting tour aboard the *Frances*, a seventy-four-foot gaff-top cutter. With cushioned benches and sides higher than most sailing schooners, the guests are less likely to find themselves overboard due to wind, sea, or wine.

"Wine is about exploring and being adventurous," Archer says of the nautical tastings. "I purposefully try to not have the same wine twice so the tastings are as unpredictable as the weather. However, we won't sail in bad weather and we won't drink bad wine!"

The two-hour voyage from Maine State Pier also educates about Portland, sea life, and sailing history for interested passengers, even allowing honorary deckhands the chance to hoist a sail or pilot the ship.

Frances's owner, Megan Jones, expertly sails her, allowing connoisseurs to comfortably tack through Casco Bay's islands within toasting distance of three prominent lighthouses. Even dedicated teetotallers may join their friends in the fun.

Departs at Maine Sailing Adventures at Maine State Pier
207-619-4630
winewiseevents.com

EAT LIKE A LOCAL
AT HARVEST ON THE HARBOR

"Harvest on the Harbor is nothing less than a Food Euphoria," WLOB radio host Ray Richardson tells listeners when describing Maine's multi-day food festival. "I'm a a big guy, and I know food! There is nothing like this anywhere else in the world."

Set in breathtaking locations around Portland's working waterfront in fall, events take place at venues ranging from industrial chic to modern sleek. More than two thousand people soak in harbor panoramas while sampling beer, wine, spirits, and fine cuisine from as many as sixty top culinary offerings around the state.

The culinary extravaganza's signature Maine Lobster Chef of the Year competition is a selective juried tasting of the state's most creative *Homarus americanus* preparation. To qualify, chefs are nominated, selected, and in some cases advance as winners from other lobster-festival contests in Maine. The winner receives state bragging rights and understandably packs their dining room for the following year.

For a comprehensive Maine food experience, foodies attend the Marketplace weekend session. Always presented in large venues, the popularity outgrew itself in the first year, and now events are hosted in several restaurants and venues around the city to comfortably accommodate droves of foodies.

harvestontheharbor.com

● ●

THAI CHILI SAUSAGE
ON THE THIRSTY PIG'S BACK DECK

On a pleasant day, kick back with a beer on the back deck of The Thirsty Pig. Overlooking the castle-like grandeur of the former armory is reason enough to be there. Pair that beer with the Thai chili sausage sandwich and the experience is complete.

The Exchange Street eatery is a surprise, specializing in a variety of pork sausage offerings—and an impressive lineup it is. The Thai chili stands out as a flavorful selection that has enough spiciness to enhance the taste without overpowering or searing the palate. If you catch it right, a skilled beer-sommelier-like bartender will know the perfect pint to pair. Choosing which beer will best complement the specific flavors of each sausage is truly an art form.

37 Exchange St., 207-773-2469
thirstypigportland.com

NOTE
There are a couple of menu items to stave off a vegetarian veto if dining with friends.

LOBSTER TACO
AT THE HIGHROLLER LOBSTER CO.

Portland is known for lobster, and more than that, lobster rolls, but lobster tacos . . . not so much.

But do not confuse owners Andy Gerry and Baxter Key's innovative twist on a lobster roll with a Tex-Mex fave. After starting their crustacian-themed food-cart in 2015, the pair discovered melted cheese that accidently spilled over onto their sizzling flat top quickly congealed. Taking it to the next level, they began creating larger controlled crispy cheese, and loaded the folded Cheesy Bacon Taco Shells with fresh Maine lobster meat, topped with vegetables, drizzled with homemade red pepper and jalapeño mayo.

The off-the-menu innovation quickly caught on with regulars at the curb-side cart in the Old Port, becoming a viral sensation on Thrillist. The sudden demand catapulted the streetside kitchen to a brick-and-mortar eatery in the Old Port. Loyal to the locals that brought them the unexpected success, Gerry and Key kept the food cart operation, as well.

104 Exchange St.
highrollerlobster.com

Cart: outside The Custom House, 70 Commercial St.

The true Maine lobster roll: generous portion of lobster meat (two tails and four claws), lettuce, a dollop of mayonnaise, all on a toasted hot dog roll (drawn butter instead of mayo if served hot).

Other unique lobster rolls:

The Porthole Restaurant & Pub

Eventide

Joe's Smoke Shop

Scales

Street & Co.

ALL-YOU-CAN-EAT FISH-AND-CHIPS
AT THE PORTHOLE

"To the Porthole!" exclaims Old Orchard Beach native Michael Ruoss. "It's our battle cry." Ruoss, now a New Orleans chef, enjoys the popular waterfront restaurant and pub perched on Custom House Wharf whenever he's home. If it happens to be a Friday, then the all-you-can-eat fish-and-chips is on the menu! Served with french fries and cole slaw, the Shipyard Beer-battered fish is overly generous. If a customer is really hungry—just coming back from a week at sea or hasn't eaten all day—a second helping might be in order. If a third is needed . . . well, who cares? It's all-you-can-eat!

The Porthole opened in 1929, and has managed to retain its authentic working-waterfront charm for more than eighty-five years. Media try to capture its Maine mystique, as the Porthole pops up in car commercials and Tommy Hilfiger fashion catalogs. The interior has been called "harbor-chic," with uneven floors, a long counter, and views of the wharf. An expansive deck offers highboy seating as well as picnic benches. A blind seal the staff calls "Sylvester" frequents the water below, instinctively knowing where the food is. But while looking for him, a seagull may drop in and stare you down for the leftovers!

20 Custom House Wharf, 207-773-4653

portholemaine.com

TANDOORI CHICKEN
AT MISTER BAGEL (DOWNTOWN)

All Mister Bagels in Maine are not created equal. As a franchise, the locations wisely are allowed to tweak their menus to appeal to their location, location, location. Rash Sandhu's downtown location embraces its cosmopolitan customers—as well as Sandhu's culture—with menu items unique to this bagel shop, including his signature tandoori panini.

Originally from Punjab and educated in England, Sandhu keeps the surrounding art college students and office workers walking extra blocks for dishes other Mister Bagels don't have. Ignore any heavy sighs or eye rolls with the extra work that goes into creating the panini—the smell alone will ease feeling a little guilty for inconveniencing the overwhelmed staff during lunch rush. The first bite will completely eliminate any guilt.

"I am not a foodie—no way," Sandhu says. "I like experimenting, and being able to add a little of my own culture is fun."

Spicy both in flavor and heat, it's moderate enough to not dissuade those with milder taste, but enough to keep fans of Punjabi cuisine eating more.

539 Congress St., 207-774-8582

TAP THE KEGS
AT THE SHIPYARD BREWERY

While dozens of breweries have sprouted up around the metro area over the past decade, many winning prestigious awards, Shipyard Brewing Company's factory looms in the East End as a living monument of the neighborhood's working-class roots. The brewery is open for beer lovers to take free tours daily, roam the extensive gift shop, and taste the numerous brands made on premises. Shipyard's line of Captain Eli's flavored Root Beers allows the tour and tastings to be a family experience.

When Shipyard opened in 1994, there were few craft beers being made. But Portland's rising tide in culinary arts has lifted the other craft-beer ships, or rather, glasses—and the city has developed into something of a beer town, recognized by *USA Today* as one of the "Top 10 Beer Towns" in 2014.

Never one to coast, owner Fred Forsley has jumped into the city's distilling boom by introducing Ice Pik Vodka.

86 Newbury St., 207-761-0807
shipyard.com

TIP
Although the Shipyard Brewery doesn't have dining on premises, you can eat at their nom de plume restaurants: The Inn on Peaks Island, The Sea Dog Microbrewery (South Portland, Topsham), and Federal Jack's (Kennebunk).

CRAFT BREWERIES IN PORTLAND

Austin Street Brewery, 1 Industrial Way

Bissell Brothers Brewing Co., 4 Thompsons Point

Allagash Brewing Co., 50 Industrial Way

Battery Steele Brewing, 1 Industrial Way

Lone Pine Brewing Co., 219 Anderson St.

Foundation Brewing Co., 1 Industrial Way

Goodfire Brewing Co., 219 Anderson St.

Rising Tide Brewing Co.,103 Fox St.

Liquid Riot Bottling Co., 250 Commercial St.

Wash Ashore Beer Co., 110 Marginal Way

Peak Organic Brewing Co., 110 Marginal Way

Sebago Brewing Co., 211 Fore St.

Bunker Brewing Co., 17 Westfield St.

One Eye Open Brewing Co., 41 Fox St.

D.L. Geary Brewing Co., 38 Evergreen Dr.

Casco Bay Brewing Co., 57 Industrial Way

Gritty McDuff's Brewing Co., 396 Fore St.

LOBSTER GARLIC SMASHED POTATOES
AT DIAMOND'S EDGE

By the time you realize the lawn overlooking the dock on Great Diamond Island is shaped like a martini glass, its clear Diamond Cove (a.k.a: Cocktail Cove) will be the ideal spot for a Diamond's Edge aperitif. On the grounds of former Fort McKinley, the Diamond's Edge Restaurant & Marina is accessible by Casco Bay Lines ferry or private craft. Nestled in the island's quiet side, the patio and indoor tables gaze out to the boats sailing Hussey Sound's nautical highway and Long Island across the channel.

The scenic summer spot's real draw, however, is the food with a view—particularly the Lobster Garlic Smashed Potatoes. The menu is understandably seafood heavy, but features eclectic American fare, including natural chicken breast, a BBQ pork rib, and Black & Blue Filet Mignon. But all the items seem incomplete without Diamond's Edge's signature side dish. Artfully prepared with Maine's famous crustacean, it's a perfect Portland complement to any entrée or sandwich. Ordering it alone isn't a bad idea either.

1 Diamond Ave., Great Diamond Island, 207-766-5850
diamondsedgerestaurantandmarina.com

EAT, JUST BECAUSE
AT FORE STREET RESTAURANT

Just eat at Fore Street. Anything. That's it.

It really doesn't matter what it is because it will be excellent. And if one does catch an off night (never heard of one, but we'll go with the possibility), Chef Sam Hayward and his staff will ensure it is corrected. Wait staff have been known to suggest visitors from Manhattan select another dish rather than relaying an order for a very well-done prime rib. Invariably, they'll eat the prime rib medium loving every bite.

Portland's explosion on the food scene may be recent, but one of the original fuses is the converted-industrial brick restaurant on its Old Port namesake street. It isn't a waterfront eatery, it doesn't have great views, and there is no deck to escape the loud dimly lit dining room, but there's no reason to. The food is exceptional.

Since opening in the summer of 1996, Fore Street has been continually recognized by culinary publications, blogs, and the James Beard Foundation, including Hayward's award as Outstanding Chef, Northeast—making Hayward the very first chef in Maine to capture the prestigious honor. Topping culinary lists internationally, the restaurant also impresses with a knowledgeable and efficient wait staff that ensures the presentation equals the cuisine.

If full, try Hayward's more recent contribution to the seafood scene, Scales, a mere wharf away.

288 Fore St., 207-775-2717
forestreet.biz

BE DRIVEN TO DRINK
BY THE MAINE BREW BUS

It's not difficult to spot the distinctive bright green school buses looping around the city, delivering thirsty Zythophiles to safely experience three to four craft breweries with tours of the facilities as well as the history of the labels. Enthusiasts love tasting special batches in testing phases, and being the first to taste an impending craze.

With the proliferation of breweries in the area (more than 50 in the metro area, with well over a dozen in Portland's city limits alone—and more popping up all the time), responsible education and enjoyment of the craft beer scene was identified early in the craze by Zach Poole while contemplating the Maine beer scene at Novare Res. He and his wife and Allison revved up Maine Brew Bus in 2012, purchasing fifteen-seat "Lenny" on craigslist from the Kennebunk School Department.

The bus tours travel to tastings at an alternating series of breweries, while guides present libatious stories related to Portland's alcohol-laced history, from being the birthplace of Prohibition to Rum Riots to being the childhood home of Hollywood's greatest directors—yes, it actually relates!

Since its creation, the Brew Bus has expanded to many more buses and includes tours in Massachusetts and Rhode Island, as well, never deviating from their slogan "We drive you to drink locally."

79 Commercial St., 207-200-9111
themainebrewbus.com

GARLIC CHICKEN PIE
AT PIZZA VILLA

"It's our signature pie—everybody loves it," says Jo Martin of Pizza Villa's best-selling garlic chicken creation. "It's always been there."

The ten-inch pizza starts with white-meat chicken chunks sautéed in garlic and olive oil. The meat is mixed with chopped spinach and feta cheese and baked to consistent perfection in minutes. The flavors hit the roof of the mouth before the first bite is even taken, and then let the eating begin.

If traditionalists are not ready to go so garlic all at once, "you can get half of the pie chicken and garlic, and the other half cheese and pepperoni," Martin reassures. "People can't decide, so we do it all the time."

When asked why his sought-after pizza only comes in ten-inch pies, owner Phil Regis always laughs, "I got a good deal on the pans in the '60s."

940 Congress St., 207-774-1777

EGGS BENEDICT
AT HOT SUPPA

"I would be a vegan, but can't do it as long as Hot Suppa has their Fried Green Tomato Eggs Benedict," says regular Steff Deschenes. "Oh my God, the Fried Green Tomato! Yeah, not going to happen."

The pint-sized eatery just outside Longfellow Square is a West End favorite and often has lines out the door for any meal. Brothers Moses and Alec Sabina wanted to present a solid representation of "American classics" inspired by their culinary exploration largely south of the Mason-Dixon line. Spicy and flavorful, the poached eggs over an English muffin with hollandaise sauce and choice of meat (or tomatoes) are served with fresh fruit and Geechie Boy grits or hashbrowns.

Putting a Maine twist on southern fare, the dishes are a seamless fusion of great seafood and fresh produce.

703 Congress St., 207-871-5005
hotsuppa.com

- - - - - - - - - - (21) - - - - - - - - - - -

WINE IN A BLIZZARD
AT MJ'S WINE BAR

"Welcome to life inside the snow globe," says MJ's owner Mark Ohlson as guests stomp off the accumulating snow in the downtown bar. Its expansive walls of glass open to views of swirling flakes throughout City Center into Lobsterman Park and Canal Plaza beyond.

MJ's Wine Bar (and let's be clear here—wine only!), named after Ohlson's mother, Mary Jane, is a large space with a welcoming U-shaped bar, back tables, and a lounge area with plush leather couches defying you to leave. If the piano's ivories are being tickled or a jazz trio performs—baby, it's cold outside!—it may take a dogsled rescue to actually get someone to leave.

"While I have lived in the beautiful wine regions of France, Spain, New Zealand, and California, [Portland] is still my home," Ohlson shares in his online love letter. And he clearly likes having people over.

If a snowstorm hits Portland the third Thursday in November, MJ's Beaujolais Nouveau Day party will be even more legen—wait for it—dary!

1 City Center, 207-772-1400
onecitywines.com

TIP
A great spot in all seasons, MJ's Wine Bar has a large patio for summertime sips outside and features a year-round waffle brunch on Sundays.

REAL ITALIANS
AT AMATO'S

Not all sandwiches are created equal, nor should they be. There's little point in getting a cheesesteak outside the Philadelphia city limits, po'boys belong in New Orleans, New York is for heroes, and grinders are Boston, but Italians are all Portland.

Like the other sandwiches, there is a story behind the name, and it starts with Giovanni Amato in 1902. An Italian immigrant (made the connection yet?), Amato started selling rolls stuffed with meat and veggies to Portland's waterfront workers from a cart. His first store on India Street still thrives and the business has more than forty shops in the northeast.

Amato's lists "Amato's Original" Italian consisting of "ham, American cheese, onion, pickle, tomato, green pepper, olive, salt and pepper, and oil." Though the Original is Amato's most popular sandwich, some swap the core ingredients for a more Italian combination of Genoa salami, capicola, prosciutto, and provolone. Non-traditionalists opt for turkey, roast beef, pepperoni, tuna salad, chicken salad, or—say it ain't so, Giovanni!—veggie Italians.

Regardless of any affinity one might have for another region's sandwich, Amato's Italian is definitively Portland and it needs to be tried.

Original shop: 71 India St., 207-773-1682
amatos.com

STEP BACK IN TIME
IN THE MISS PORTLAND DINER

The Worcester Lunch Car Company's 1949 Miss Portland Diner seems remarkably out of place among the new construction and high rises shooting up around it in its Bayside neighborhood. And that iconic irony evokes a smile from owner Tom Manning.

A Portland native, Manning grew up on Munjoy Hill with the diner a constant throughout his childhood. The vintage diner even made a cameo in Mel Gibson's film, *Man Without a Face*. When the retiring owner was unable to sell the classic car, he gave it to the city so it would not be destroyed.

After retiring from 35 years in New York City magazine publishing, Manning purchased it from the city in 2007 and returned to his home town to oversee its restoration along with the city's historic preservation department. Reopening in 2008 restored with meticulous detail to its historical integrity, it is Portland's only landmark diner in a new location on Marginal Way and enlarged with an expanded kitchen as well as an additional dining area in case the booths and stools are full up. Manning did not stop with the building, however, and created a menu that equally reflected the traditional diner fare while rising to the culinary standards expected from Portland's foodies.

Order up!

140 Marginal Way, 207-210-6673
missportlanddiner.com

LFK BURGER
IN LONGFELLOW SQUARE

There is no way to describe how much this is not "just another burger." On the paper menu, it reads pretty basic, but the unexpected explosion of flavor makes this one of the top burgers you may ever eat.

Topped with pimento cheese, bacon, and garlic mayo on a buttery roll, the juicy hand-made Classic LFK Burger is more than memorable. Unless you request otherwise, it's automatically prepared a perfect medium-rare and served with bacon-sprinkled potato salad that has a hint of vinaigrette.

LFK is unique. Fashioned a writer's bar, Longfellow's influence is impossible to ignore. The Longfellow Square location even has Longo's statue looming outside an oversize plate-glass window. Inspiration is in the woodwork—literally—as bar rails are supported by typewriter keys (spelling out Emily Dickinson's poem "After great pain, a formal feeling comes"). A vintage Woodstock and Smith-Corona sit in cubbies. Blank paper waits at the ready above the antique typewriters for any aspiring Hemingways eager to start their novel before their burger is finished. It's the kind of place that actually finds one wishing for Longfellow's famous lament—"The day is cold, and dark, and dreary"—as an excuse to stay longer and order again.

188A State St., 207-899-3277
facebook.com/LFKportland

PIEDMONTESE BEEF
AT PORTLAND REGENCY HOTEL & SPA

Regardless if the craving is for a filet mignon, New York sirloin, tenderloin carpaccio, taco salad, or just a burger, this Old Port luxe hotel (reimagined in the city's former armory) has three very different dining experiences to pair with their superior Piedmontese beef. From the hotel's private farm, the meat is "known for its high protein content while being lower in fat and cholesterol than turkey." And it's delicious.

Twenty Milk Street's wood-panelled ceiling evokes the quiet pre-hipster elegance of the Oak Room, with a brick fireplace and a cozy table in the front turret. "I keep trying Fore Street [restaurant], but I just like it here more," says Portland Symphony Orchestra flautist Alison Hale at her pre-concert haunt. "Really, it's just my favorite place!"

Live music can often be heard here and while the entertainment varies, it's frequently (and appropriately) jazz standards.

20 Milk St., 207-774-4200
theregency.com

DARK CHOCOLATE SEA SALT DOUGHNUT
AT THE HOLY DONUT

"The dark chocolate sea salt outsells anything else we have," says Exchange Street clerk Alison of the Holy Donut creation. "We can't keep enough around." And the popular Portland doughnut shop has only become more sought-after since the first edition.

The Holy Donut was a taste sensation in Portland before the doors ever opened. Excitement was driven by Leigh Kellis's take on the traditional doughnut that is definitively Portland—made with mashed Maine potatoes.

Instantly celebrated by national media, the original Parkside shop began rolling out innovative flavors, but the dark chocolate and sea salt flew off the racks faster than Kellis could make them—literally.

Offering something for everyone, many doughnuts are gluten-free, and there are even select vegan offerings. Egg-free cinnamon sugared and fresh berry glazed vegan doughnuts don't compromise on flavor. Don't be fooled by the primary ingredient—The Holy Donut's pastries defy density and are flaky.

Whether the choice is the original Parkside shop, the Old Port location, or a Scarborough location, get there early. While they stay open until doughnuts run out, that's rarely past 3 p.m.

194 Park Ave., 207-874-7774
7 Exchange St., 207-775-7776
theholydonut.com

MAINE FOODIE TOURS
THROUGH DOWNTOWN

The challenge in a foodie destination like Portland is twofold: how to sample all the great food and how not to put on the pounds doing it. Pam Laskey introduced her simultaneous solution to Portland in 2008 with Maine Foodie Tours. The two-and-a-half-hour stroll stops at over a half dozen notable shops and restaurants, allowing guilt-free tastings of several offerings at each location.

Partnering with some of the most delectable eateries downtown, the culinary tours mostly amble through Portland's wharves and Old Port while sampling locally sourced lobster, crab, fish, wines, and confections. The tours are led by guides who explain the city's farm-to-table movement as well as storied history. Surprisingly, they are all interlocked in unimagined ways.

Beyond the original Culinary Walking Tours, Laskey's tours have expanded with the scope of the city's culinary appeal. There are more than a dozen daily tours, some touching on the creative arts, the harbor's nautical allure, as well as a burgeoning food scene dominating the Washington Street corridor. Most will leave you stuffed, others just full enough to keep going. Maine Foodie Tours are also available in Kennebunkport, Bar Harbor, Ogunquit, and Rockland/Camden.

Tours start locations differ, 207-233-7485
mainefoodietours.com

TOUR DE FORCE

Niche culinary tours also uncover culturally related aspects of Portland:

Old Port Walking Tour

E.E.A.T.T.
(East End Artisan Tasting Tour)

Old Port Happy Hour Tour

Sherpa Tour

Lunch & Aquacultue Cruise
on Casco Bay

Fun-filled Progressive Dinners

Old Port Lobster Crawl

The Culinary Palette
Art Culture and Food Tour

Maine Lobster Picnic and Portland
Harbor Cruise

Portland Harbor Cruise and
Happy Hour Tour

GET YELLED AT
IN MARCY'S DINER

Marcy's Diner has been hiding in plain sight amid Arts District storefronts since 1989. A throwback to your grandparents' morning spot, it's wildly popular with locals, millennials, and Maine College of Art students nearby. Decked out with Americana memorabilia and vintage signs, the diner is as irreverent as it is delicious.

Marcy's opens early for breakfast and closes after the lunch crowd dissipates. Lunches are good, but breakfast is the reason to go. The tiny downtown diner takes no reservations and only accepts cash. Expect to be one of the few patrons to not be greeted by name. Wait staff are not unpleasant as much as crazy busy, so take no offense if a smile is not immediately available—and don't plan on getting one if children are ill-behaved!

Never known for tolerating disruptive patrons of any sort, owner Darla Neugebauer made international news in July 2015 when she loudly reprimanded a two-year-old whose tantrum was going unheeded by the parents for in excess of twenty minutes in the tiny diner. The resulting media frenzy had two results: families with undisciplined children avoid the place, people who do not like being subjected to bad parenting pack the place. Win Win.

Make sure to pick up a "I Got Yelled at in Marcy's Diner" T-shirt and bumper sticker!

47 Oak St., 207-774-9713
nicemuffin.com

PORTLAND BREAKFAST FAVES

Portland Pottery Café

118 Washington Ave., 207-245-6335
portlandpottery.com

Hot Suppa

703 Congress St., 207-871-5005
hotsuppa.com

Miss Portland Diner

40 Marginal Way, 207-210-6673,
missportlanddiner.com

The Porthole Restaurant & Pub

20 Custom House Wharf, 207-773-4653,
portholemaine.com

Ruski's Restaurant & Pub

212 Danforth St., 207-774-7604

TABLE NUMBER 7
AT BACK BAY GRILL

Anticipating a revitalized Bayside area three decades too early, Back Bay Grill serves epicurean fantasies with unrelenting excellence. One of the few truly white-table cloth restaurants in a city famous for casual comfort, the restaurant is an elegant stalwart for romance and fine dining.

And while chatting with chefs and bartenders on the counter, and window seats looking into Bubba's line of Pat Benatars and Madonnas waiting to dance across the street are enjoyable, Table 7 is the best of the best. Purported to be the most requested "best seat in the house," the corner banquette offers intimate seclusion with discreet sightlines to the bar and open kitchen.

The menu changes daily, but there is often a signature duck entrée that should be seriously considered by one-time patrons, although there really are no bad choices.

While not bantered about by passing foodies onto "the newest hotspot," its snug dining room is a consistent favorite with locals and fills fast, so get a reservation! Life is too short.

65 Portland St., 207-772-8833
backbaygrill.com

FRENCH FRIES
AT DUCKFAT

This gourmet sandwich shop opened in the East End in 2005, intent on making sure the unappealing name explains it all. Believed to be among the healthiest of animal fats for cooking, the flavorful base is the reason eyeballs roll in ecstasy to the back of diners' heads. Of all the offerings, Duckfat's Belgian fries consistently evoke that emotion.

Nancy Pugh and Rob Evans know the appeal of their side dish, often ordered as a nonshared entrée, and don't pull punches about it. They flatly state, "Hand-cut Maine potatoes, fried Belgian-style in duck fat, tossed with our seasoning salt and served . . . with your choice of eight homemade dipping sauces—these fries are our inspiration and the reason we opened Duckfat." Sauces include garlic mayo, lemon-herb mayo, truffle ketchup, horseradish mayo, Thai-chili mayo, and toasted curry mayo with a nominal additional fee.

Unpretentious, the restaurant does not take reservations, and tight quarters make for long lines at peak hours. Some might ask if it's worth the wait, but the answer is with the regulars at the back of the line.

43 Middle St., 207-774-8080
duckfat.com

JENGA CARROTS
AT BOLSTER, SNOW, & CO.

While not officially named after the popular game of teetering interlaced blocks, it's not difficult to understand the reference when these intricately stacked carrot fries are artfully presented to patrons at Bolster, Snow & Company. Executive Chef Nicholas Verdisco's creation is expertly complemented with a curry mayo blue cheese dip, and will even appeal to those who think they hate carrots.

"I wanted them to stand out—be different—not just fried in a cup," says Verdisco. "I wanted to utilize horse carrots being wasted. But they aren't the most aesthetically pleasing vegetable, so I stacked them like Lincoln Logs, and they are a hit."

The Francis Hotel in the 1881 Mellen E. Bolster House is listed on the National Park Service's Registry of Historic Places. The elegant restaurant's name is a nod to a business once run by the mansion's former owner, designer Francis Fassett.

Verdisco's innovative menu "is fiercely seasonal and heavily influenced by relationships with local purveyors, farmers, and producers."

747 Congress St., 207-772-7496
bolstersnow.com

OKTOBERFEST
AT NOVARE RES

Tucked behind the bustling shops of Middle and Exchange streets is Novare Res Bier Café—an oasis where beer lovers can hide while loved ones shop. The stone and brick interior is dimly lit even on the brightest of days and practically screams "Welgekomen!" as you enter.

Latin for "to start a revolution," Novare Res owners Eric and Julie Michaud pledge "a beer drinking revolution . . . [striving] to serve what we feel are the best beers legally available to us in the state of Maine combined with the determination to try to support the small craft movement all over the world."

Despite protests of "not trying to be a German biergarten," the outdoor patio and selection of expertly crafted draught brews from the fatherland make little difference come Oktoberfest. The bar honors the feast by pouring limited styles of bier in one-liter "maas" based on Munich's celebration (typically the last weekend in September or first weekend in October).

Durstig yet?

4 Canal Plaza, 207-761-2437
novareresbiercafe.com

MUSIC AND ENTERTAINMENT

SHAKESPEARE IN THE PARK
BY FENIX THEATRE COMPANY

Friends, Portlanders, countrymen, lend them your ears! Fenix Theatre Company will make you laugh, cry, and cheer as they present the plays—both comedic and tragic—of William Shakespeare in the natural beauty of Deering Oaks Park.

For those who find The Bard dry, these free performances bringing his characters to life are more than worth the cost of admission. The troupe's energy and talent engage audiences emotionally as well as physically. Taking the famous "All the world's a stage . . ." line to a new level, cast members pop up throughout the Frederick Law Olmsted-designed park, interacting around and with the audience.

If iambic pentameter isn't your cup of tea, the troupe occasionally deviates to interpreting other playwrights, including Anton Chekhov and Samuel Beckett.

Shows are Thursday, Friday, and Saturday evenings in July and August. There are no seats, so bring a blanket or folding chair. Many audience members bring a picnic to the play. Also remember gobs of DEET for the mosquitoes.

Deering Oaks Park Ravine, 207-400-6223
fenixtheatre.com

JAY YORK CONCERTS
IN BAYSIDE

Entering the 1916 grange-style church on the downhill slope leading to Portland's Back Cove, you suddenly realize two things: the eclectic musical lineups are anything but ecclesiastical, and you're actually in someone's living room. Jay York's Last Church on the Left is literally that, at the bottom of the one-block street in the shadow of Maine's tallest building.

York bought the former church from the Moonies in 1990 and creatively adapted the structure to serve as his in-house photography studio and home. His inspiration of opening his living-room nave to stage live concerts began as a fund-raiser for St. Lawrence Arts. Now, performances number around eight a year. Notification is by word of mouth or e-mail only. Acts come from around the world, but all donations received go "one hundred percent to the performer," says York.

As a low-income and blue-collar industrial part of downtown, Bayside is going through a gentrification that is both welcomed and vilified by polarized segments of the community. York's contribution to Portland's performing arts skillfully walks a tightrope by feeding the aspirations of the creative economy while maintaining enough of a bohemian low-profile approach to not ruffle neighborhood feathers.

58 Wilmot St., 207-773-3434
facebook.com/events/618054454951884

MAGIC OF CHRISTMAS
AT PORTLAND SYMPHONY ORCHESTRA

When the conductor emerges from the wings of Merrill Auditorium in his red Santa hat, the tone is literally set for Portland Symphony Orchestra's traditional holiday concert series two weeks in December.

"The PSO has been performing the Magic of Christmas for more than 35 years," says Director of Education and Community Engagement John Elliot.

As the baton turns to strike up the band, every musician is donning antlers, flashing hats, red reindeer noses, elf ears, or another nod to the season. The jingling bells elicit a cheer as the PSO takes the audience on its annual Sleigh Ride, complete with simulated cracking whip.

While truly a concert celebrating the wonder of the Christian holiday, the Symphony does an excellent job of not alienating other faiths by accentuating and educating. In expounding on the magic of the season, conductors present the significance and influence of the music and traditions shared throughout western cultures. The conductors expertly explain the relevance of Christmas to the works of classical composers and contemporary pop culture, in an inclusive manner, devoid of condescension, honoring the significance of the holiday for the faithful and children in the audience.

Try not singing during the Christmas Carol sing-a-long . . . I double-dog dare you.

20 Myrtle St., 207-842-0800
porttix.com

DANCE IN THE STREETS
AT THE OLD PORT FESTIVAL

Like nowhere else, the Old Port Festival welcomes the warm weather to Portland's downtown the second weekend in June during the city's Summer Kickoff Weekend. The waterfront district is alive with multiple stages (rock, country, folk, and more) and food vendors all catering to musical and culinary tastes of all kinds. A single-day event for almost five decades, the festival has expanded into a weekend event including working waterfront tours, city discovery competitions, and the Casco Bay Eye, a ninety-foot Ferris wheel with commanding views of the city and harbor.

Live performances are sprinkled throughout the neighborhood's city streets and parks. Free entertainment is widespread with dancing, juggling, comedy, and cirque-styled aerial aerobatics.

The festival performances and concerts are all free, but food vendors and rides often have fees.

The Old Port Exchange District, 207-772-6828
portlandmaine.com/old-port-festival/

STUMBLE ALONG
WHARF STREET

"Dining out on the cobbles, beneath flickering, period gas lamps is an agreeable faux-time travel experience," says *USA Today* of Wharf Street's romantic nineteenth-century atmosphere, naming it one of the top 10 Prettiest Cobblestone Streets Across America. Amid the shops, restaurants, nightclubs, and cocktail lounges, people are often seen losing their footing on the uneven pavers whether it be due to the high heels or highballs.

Closed to vehicles during evenings, all ages are represented walking the thoroughfare. Steep steps and sidewalks bring people down from the rest of the Old Port to enjoy two blocks filled with everything from upscale seafood to Giant Jenga. The street is conveniently bookended by the historic Mariners Church building with art galleries, a billiards club, and a pub on one end and the Portland Harbor Hotel on the other.

Out for a night on the town, a romantic stroll, or just there to people watch, Wharf Street has something for everyone. Just ask anyone at the Bar of Chocolate.

Spans between Moulton Place and Union Street,
parallel between Commercial and Fore streets.

THE (EVERCHANGING) LIST OF WHARF STREET BUSINESSES

Amigo's Mexican

Bar of Chocolate

Beals Old Fashioned Ice Cream

The Blazin' Ace

Bonfire

Central Provisions restaurant

Gritty McDuff's Brew Pub

Higher Grounds

Jaeger

Joseph's Men's Clothing

Mash Tun

Oasis night club

Pearl

Port Boutique

Portmanteau

Street & Co. restaurant

Vignola restaurant

'80S NIGHT
AT BUBBA'S SULKY LOUNGE

Paying the cover charge at the door into Bubba's infamous (and sulky) retro dance party every Friday night is a toll into Bayside's Twilight Zone. A Portland institution for close to fifty years, '80s Night is a (relatively) recent invention catering to those from the Brat Pack era, appropriate since Judd Nelson is a Portland native.

But the dance music from bands—some wildly popular and some even still touring—transcends the *Breakfast Club* crowd. '80s Night is timeless—or is it ageless? The disco-era dance floors (holdovers—even by Bubba's standards—from 1977's Saturday Night Fever) finds octogenarians dirty dancing with millennials. Much of the under-thirty crowd are authentic in drop-shoulder sweatshirts, teased hair, and side-ponytails.

But Bubba's is the real star here. The low-rise lounge is deceptively large inside. The venue seems shockingly endless—there are rooms, and side rooms, and sub rooms—all with vignettes of eras gone by. Two island bars bookend the building, one fronting Portland Street evokes a bus station lounge while the back bar is a lively dance oasis available for private parties. The ceiling is a hanging Guiness World Record-worthy treasure of vintage lunch boxes totally worth the cover alone. It's what TGI Friday's might have looked like had it started in Maine.

92 Portland St., 207-828-0549
bubbassulkylounge.com

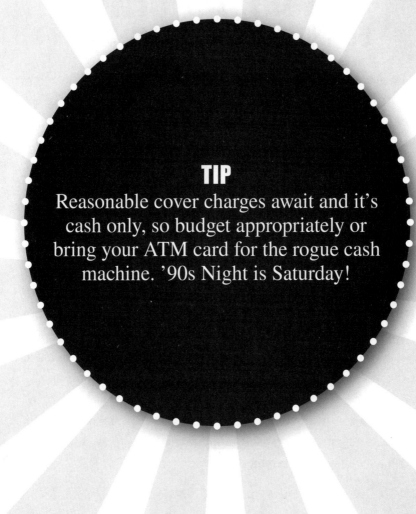

TIP

Reasonable cover charges await and it's cash only, so budget appropriately or bring your ATM card for the rogue cash machine. '90s Night is Saturday!

SUNSET CONCERTS
ON THE WESTERN PROMENADE

The sun setting over the White Mountains stretching into New Hampshire has a soundtrack when viewed from the edge of Bramhall Hill on Tuesdays during the summer. A free concert series is scheduled at various city parks for weeknights in July and August, and the Western Promenade hosts variations on folk music while the last rays disappear over Mount Washington more than seventy-five miles away.

The Western Promenade is lined with stately stone and brick mansions from the robber-baron days. The homes were built to claim enviable sight lines west. As the city expanded over the centuries, the undulating horizon's foreground was marred with Portland International Jetport and the state's largest retail mall with surrounding shopping centers. It all makes a beautiful and ironic backdrop to the music born of a counter-culture society. You almost expect Joni Mitchell to get out when a big yellow taxi pulls up.

There is something relaxing and a tad bit dizzying about the spectrum's swirl of colors splashing in the sky. It intensifies when an acoustic guitar accompanies soothing vocals in perfect harmony. Or maybe that's just the smell in the air.

Western Promenade, 207-874-8826
portlandmaine.gov

OTHER FREE CONCERTS

Wednesdays
Kids' Concerts
12:30 p.m., Deering Oaks Park

Thursdays
Jazz Concerts
7 p.m., Fort Allen Park

JULY FOURTH
ON THE EASTERN PROMENADE

On the fourth morning of July, blankets and chairs are set out on Eastern Promenade's expansive bluff as soon as the sun rises in anticipation of the Stars and Stripes Spectacular over twelve hours away. Food trucks, vendors, and police roll up to serve the masses. By evening, Munjoy Hill closes to non-resident cars clearing streets for pedestrians. Scores of boats moor in earshot of the annual concert. A respectful hush quiets 70,000 excited patriots when the Portland Pops takes the stage.

After soul-stirring tributes to America, starting with the national anthem, the conductor guides the audience through patriotic music both relevant and historical. Then, as the final embers of daylight fade, the orchestra's maestro raises goosebumps with the opening notes of Pyotr Ilyich Tchaikovsky's 1812 Overture.

Just when kids are bored by the fifteen-minute classical piece, the tempo changes, signalling its famous booming crescendo. It climaxes with pyrotechnics in place of the composer's cannon fire. As the music concludes, a full fireworks show begins. Funded by generous sponsors when city hall failed to fund the celebration, the explosions over the harbor impress with dramatic scale and duration.

Eastern Promenade
july4thportland.org

TIP

Portland's hillside makes for perfect stadium seating, but if enjoying the crowded hillside isn't your thing, VIP seating with table service is available for a premium.

Wherever you sit—no matter how early you go—remember the concert and fireworks end after dark and the car is most likely a mile or more (unlit) walk away. . . . Bring a headlamp or flashlight to navigate the uneven terrain!

SEE BOB MARLEY
...EVERYWHERE.

First of all: No, not the late reggae star. This Bob Marley is a Portland-based stand-up comic. He often personally mans his kiosk at The Maine Mall. A local celebrity, who thoroughly enjoys his loyal following, Marley appears in films and TV, most memorably as a comedic foil as an over-zealous policeman to Willem Dafoe's hyper-focused detective in The Boondock Saints films.

His humor is sometimes so localized, the punchlines almost seem like inside jokes for locals in the audience—and sometimes they are—making the confusion of flatlanders in the crowd part of the fun. But his rants on parents, family, and trying to get downtime "Upta' Camp" (Translation: Mainers heading up north to vacation homes, which are referred to as camps) are universal themes—once past the Maine accent and colloquialisms—to which everyone relates.

Bob Marley is not a hard man to find. His series of comedy CDs and DVDs are numerous. He is a spokesman for various local businesses on TV, and he is seemingly always performing somewhere. He performs at small clubs regionally, and does charity concerts for area nonprofits and schools as fundraisers, yet his holiday performance series through New Year's still consistently sells out Merrill Auditorium. People cannot seem to get enough of him. No wonder he needs to go upta' camp.

bmarley.com

ROCK AND ROLL ALL NIGHT
AT THE STATE THEATRE

Many major cities have a classic art-deco-style theater, but the State Theatre's classic motif is accented with Moorish decor, making it feel more like Casablanca than Portland. Inside the venue's performance space, 1,680 fans have enjoyed, screamed, danced, and rocked from the sweeping balcony to the mosh pit. A standing bar in the right orchestra section keeps the liquor flowing without missing a beat.

Beginning as a movie theater in 1929, the State Theatre was originally designed to have a "capacity of 2,300," relates general manager Lauren Wayne. "It operated as a first-run movie house until the late 1960s, when it became a porn theater."

After decades of fits and starts, the State finally found steady footing under Wayne's leadership with a New York City promotion and management company. With additional support from Live Nation concerts, the venue has catapulted the Arts District to new heights.

The theater has hosted great names in music. The eclectic collection of window cards includes Elvis Costello, Pat Benatar, My Morning Jacket, George Thorogood, Arctic Monkeys, Lyle Lovett, and John Hiatt.

609 Congress St., 207-956-6000
statetheatreportland.com

BE SACRED & PROFANE
AT BATTERY STEELE

On the Saturday after the harvest moon, graffiti artists, tightrope walkers, jugglers, performance artists, and admirers of all things counterculture find their way to the hidden halls of Battery Steele. Celebrating the change of seasons through the arts, commercialism is shunned in the Sacred & Profane Festival.

Overgrown with grass, shrubs, and natural fauna throughout the concrete fortification, Battery Steele isn't so much hidden as it is inconspicuous. The 1942-constructed World War II battery stands sentry on Peaks Island's eastern foreside. Brilliant depictions by some of the world's foremost street artists mix with those of locals on the vast man-made cave walls. Sculptures, installations, and performances add to the merriment as lights attempt to illuminate the "profane" creativity amid the "sacred" walls of the battery.

In keeping with the event's motif, the annual festival is not advertised or promoted. Either it's known, or it's not. Word of mouth reminds those who may not be following its pagan-based timetable.

21 Central Ave. Ext., Peaks Island

TIP

Formally known as "U.S. Army Corps of Engineers Battery Construction #102," Battery Steele is thought to be the "largest battery ever built anywhere in the United States," according to the book *An Island at War* by Kim MacIsaac and historian Joel Eastman. A grand canvas for the repressed emotions— good and bad.

NOONDAY CONCERT
AT FIRST PARISH CHURCH

Jazz and classical music wafts from Maine's oldest continually operating church Thursdays during winter though mid-April. Portland Conservatory of Music performs free concerts for a lunch-break crowd in the Unitarian Universalist's 1826 granite First Parish Church, and occasionally the main branch of Portland Public Library.

Founded in 1995, the Portland Conservatory of Music trains musicians of all ages for professional careers or simple love of music. First Parish serves as a wonderful performance space with lovely acoustics expected in a traditional meeting house. The concerts offer a unique opportunity for students to perform for an audience hungry for a springtime interlude—and lunch.

With its congregational roots going back to 1632, the current 1826 church replaced its wooden 1740 predecessor known as Old Jerusalem in the same spot. Retaining the previous steeple tower, clock, bell, and Shem Drowne weathervane, the transition between the houses of worship also brought the discovery of a cannon ball from the 1775 British destruction of the city (Old Jerusalem had not otherwise been damaged). The munition is now incorporated in the church's chandelier. Maximize the experience by enjoying the school's musical interlude from the Longfellow pew where Henry Wadsworth's family attended services.

425 Congress St., 207-773-5747
firstparishportland.org

HEAR A SILENT MOVIE
WITH THE KOTZSCHMAR ORGAN

Seeing a black-and-white silent movie filling Merrill Auditorium's massive old-school silver screen creates an overwhelming sense of nostalgia. When the music emanates from the pipes of the Kotzschmar Organ, the reverberations make the age before "talkies" a tangible reality.

Portland's premier performance space turns itself over to Hollywood's two-dimensional art form, but the real star of the show is the massive 6,862-pipe organ, the second-largest in the world when installed in 1912. It was named after Hermann Kotzschmar, the incomparable organist at First Parish Church when the instrument was gifted to the city by *Saturday Evening Post* publisher Cyrus H. K. Curtis (whose middle initials represented the close family friend for whom he had been named).

Friends of the Kotzschmar Organ shows several famous films from the silent era in Merrill Auditorium, but the Halloween screenings are the most fun, particularly Lon Chaney's over-the-top and completely appropriate Phantom of the Opera (1925). When the silent movie is married with the Kotzschmar's sound, it's tempting to scan the balconies for the masked figure with his sweeping cape.

20 Myrtle St., 207-553-4363
foko.org

ALL THAT JAZZ
AT PORT CITY BLUE

Blue is a little nightclub in the Arts District with all the trappings of a Greenwich Village venue . . . without the high prices and crazy crowds. Shoehorned between a cluster of bohemian shops and restaurants, the eclectic musical performances are pure Portland. The narrow bar serves wine and beer accompanied by a small plates menu for folks as they squeeze at long tables. The name is deceptive—no one genre is represented. Samuel James will appear for some guitar rifts bemoaning an atmospheric Delta Blues. He can be followed by Rob Syvain's foot-stomping Acadian Aces whose energetic French-Canadian tunes are so deeply ingrained into Maine's heritage. Or even a country showcase. There are long-standing lineups like Wednesday night's nod to Irish music, but the weekends belong to jazz. Saturday nights feature three acts, 6 p.m. until midnight. On Sunday afternoons, a jazz jam invites anyone on stage to join the band—but they need to bring their own instrument, or voice. The songbook runs the gamut from classics to contemporary.

Mondays deviate to the spoken word with the "Worst Day of the Week" comedy showcase, which, sadly given the quality of the talent, makes the title unfortunately accurate.

650A Congress St., 207-774-4111
portcityblue.com

WALK CONGRESS STREET
ON FIRST FRIDAY ART WALK

It's one thing to walk along Congress Street sneaking peeks at new art work in galleries. It's quite another to take over Congress Street, turning the city's major downtown thoroughfare into the state's grandest open studio tour. Portland Downtown teams up with Creative Portland to ensure patrons of the arts get to experience the creative lairs of working artists, dodging in and out of gallery openings (pass the wine and cheese, please), and indulge in live performances every first Friday of the month.

The monthly stroll is anchored on One Longfellow Square in the shadow of favorite-son poet Henry Wadsworth Longfellow's statue, spanning the city's Congress Street spine through the Portland Museum of Art (open free) and State Theatre Building studios in Congress Square, past the Maine College of Art and Institute of Contemporary Art, and down to the public library's gleaming main branch at Monument Square. Beyond free admission to artists' receptions, open studio tours, and several art museums, the entire boulevard becomes a stage with entertaining street performers, musicians, acrobatics, fashion shows, theater performances, dancers, circus performers, and an occasional flash mob mixing in with the roving audience.

First Friday Art Walks are rain, or shine (or snow) year round.

Congress Street from Congress Square to Monument Square
207-370-4784
liveworkportland.org/arts/walk

• •

SPORTS AND RECREATION

CARRIAGE RIDE
THROUGH THE OLD PORT

After the city's fifty-foot holiday tree is lit, horses pull carriage rides through the Old Port every half hour on weekends between Thanksgiving and Christmas. Children are excited to experience a piece of rural nostalgia in Maine's largest urban setting, and holiday shoppers are happy to sit for a while as they ride along the city streets soaking in the holiday spirit.

Starting in Monument Square, the horses lead holiday revelers into the Old Port, down by Exchange Street's shops, past Fore Street's clubs, and return through the financial district, with a final turn at First Parish Church before gathering more passengers at the base of Portland's 1891 Soldiers and Sailors Monument.

These free trips down Portland's memory lane are a tradition sponsored by Portland's Downtown District. The organization's goal of enhancing the downtown experience for holiday shoppers has inspired several events designed to lure people away from suburban shopping, even for a little while, and to remind them of the joys of silver bells in the city.

Monument Square, 207-772-6828
portlandmaine.com

CATCH A LOBSTER
ON LUCKY CATCH CRUISES

Experience the ins and outs of catching your own lobster dinner on Lucky Catch Cruises. The ninety-minute voyage launches from Long Wharf and is led by experienced lobster man Captain Tom Martin. Lucky Catch passengers are excited to don bright orange protective gear in order to bait and haul traps, with an option to buy (at boat price) any acceptable-sized lobsters they catch—a business model believed to have been created by Tom Sawyer while whitewashing a fence.

Captain Tom presents a brief but informative lesson on industry rules and regulations with emphasis on which catch is legal to keep.

Launched in 2007, the forty-foot lobster boat has been modified to comfortably accommodate passengers where stacks of traps would normally be stored. Those along for the ride can absorb the lessons of lobstering while taking in the picturesque Calendar Island's lighthouses and historic harbor forts. Many tours even encounter seals frolicking around the boat while seagulls circle with hungry anticipation.

170 Commercial St., 207-761-0941
luckycatch.com

TIP
When back in port, take your catch to Portland Lobster Company at the end of the wharf. They will cook it to your liking for a nominal charge so you can catch your lobster and eat it, too!

DELIVER THE MAIL
WITH CASCO BAY LINES

Legend has it that Captain John Smith explored Casco Bay before he met Pocahontas. Overwhelmed by the number of islands in the protected harbor, he communicated to the king of England that "there were as many islands in the harbor as days of the year." So the Calendar Islands were named. Some attribute this to Colonel Wolfgang William Römer, but either way, in reality the U.S. Coast Guard charts only 221 islands, some barely big enough to stand on at high tide. Several large Casco Bay island communities are within the Portland city limits.

"The ten o'clock boat's been doing that run year-round since the 1890s," boasts Larry Legere, the ferry service's unofficial historian, making it the "longest-operating freight service of its kind in the country." You can do the three-hour delivery cruise around Casco Bay and visit half a dozen islands, stopping long enough for a quick hop on the docks for a photo op. Get a glimpse of the summer cottages. If it's early enough in the day, passengers can get off one boat and explore an island before catching the next one. It's often hours between deliveries, so be prepared to relax. A water taxi can rescue those who get stranded (or bored).

If longer visits are required, Portland's Casco Bay Lines ferry service to the islands scattered about the harbor is a great way to get out on the water inexpensively no matter the weather!

56 Commercial St., 207-774-7871
cascobaylines.com

JEWELL FALLS
IN THE FORE RIVER SANCTUARY

In the heart of Portland, trails lead to a thirty-foot waterfall seemingly in the middle of nowhere. Accessible from some of the city's busiest thoroughfares, treks to the natural cataract meander at various distances in the eighty-five-acre Fore River Sanctuary, depending on the trail.

The picturesque stepped cascade of water is not as remote as it seems. In reality, Jewell Falls is only a stone's throw from residential homes in the Rosemont neighborhood. The falls are named after Tom Jewell, co-founder of Portland Trails, who also donated the land where the falls are located. While the isolated spot is enjoyable anytime of the year, the springtime Fore River runoff creates a mini Niagara Falls in the center of the city limits.

The most popular trailheads begin where Congress Street crosses the Fore River in Stroudwater (longest hike from the south) and Hillcrest Avenue off Brighton Avenue (closest hike from the north). Other starting points are at the end of Starbird Lane (east side) and Rowe Avenue (west edge), allowing access to the sanctuary trails from all sides. While other access is tempting, residential streets with convenient cul-de-sacs are often unwelcoming to the additional traffic.

Portland Trails, 207-775-2411
trails.org

LIVE A FIELD OF DREAMS
AT HADLOCK FIELD

On the final Sunday baseball game of the season, a hush comes over the sold-out crowd when a disembodied voice announces, "If you build it, they will come." A tingle of delight slides up the back of the neck as Portland Sea Dogs players slowly emerge from the corn stalks in center field in vintage uniforms—that of the New England League Portland Pilots (1946-1949). As they wander the field in a mystic manner, they break the spell as they come into the stands and shake everyone's hand!

This AA farm team for the Boston Red Sox is a fun family-affordable chance to see professional players on their way to the majors—most of the players on the 2004, 2006, and 2012 Championship Red Sox and the 2017 Championship Chicago Cubs teams paid their dues on Hadlock Field. It's even a field of dreams for the Portland-area high schools, whose home-grown talent gave the MLB infielder Ryan Flaherty and pitching ace Charlie Furbush.

For those longing for the friendly confines of Fenway, the stadium has a Maine Monster similar to Boston's famed left field Green Monster proving a valuable major league training ground.

Children of all ages get to run the bases after Sunday games making all dreams come true.

271 Park Ave., 207-879-9520
seadogs.com

If baseball isn't your sport, Portland is also
home to several other professional teams:

Maine Red Claws
(Boston Celtics G-League basketball)

Portland Exposition Building, 239 Park Ave.,
207-210-6655, maine.gleague.nba.com

The Port Authorities
(WFTDA Maine Roller Derby team)

Calamity Janes
(WFTDA Maine Roller Derby B-team)

The R.I.P. Tides
(WFTDA Maine Roller Derby C-team)

Portland Exposition Building, 239 Park Ave.,
mainerollerderby.com

Maine Mammoths
(NAL Football)

Cross Insurance Arena, 1 Civic Center Sq.
207-228-1138, mainemammoths.com

Portland Mariners
(ECHL hockey)

Cross Insurance Arena, 1 Civic Center Sq.
207-761-4368, marinersofmaine.com

Portland Boxing Club

Portland Exposition Building, 239 Park Ave.
207-761-0975, portlandboxingclub.org

ROCK, PAPER, SCISSORS
AT LINCOLN'S

Lincoln's is a cash-only speakeasy named after our 16th president whose image adorns the five-dollar bill. And as such, the Prohibition-era motif charges $5—for anything. Beer? $5. Cocktail? $5. Wine? $5. Cover for comedy night? $5. Souvenir tee shirt? $5. Everything is $5 with one notable exception: The Rock-Paper-Scissors champion tee shirt cannot be bought. The only way to get the coveted garment is to win it!

Chris Massaro brought the contest to the surreptitious Old Port sanctum, where it instantly became a Sunday night sensation. Since the time of its introduction, players come and go, but Jeff Grundy maintains the "most wins" title. The bar even offers "The Grundy" (Absolut Mandarin, soda water, with a splash of cranberry and no lime) in his honor for—you guessed it—$5.

As a pure speakeasy, Lincoln's has no advertising, no social media, no phone, not even a sign. It allows locals to have an affordable locals' haunt hidden in the heart of the pricey Old Port so tourists can't even accidentally find it. In fact, you can be standing in front of the door and not know it. So, bring your game face, a handful of bluffs, and be ready to face down rock, paper, or scissors to win your shirt.

Ask someone who knows on Market Street

PLAY BILLIARDS
IN THE PORTLAND CLUB

Walking into the second-floor billiards room at the Portland Club, it's hard not to automatically scan the room for Jackie Gleason's Minnesota Fats sipping his White Tavern whiskey before mechanically clearing the table in front of an incredulous Paul Newman. The expansive room is famed architect John Calvin Stevens's shrine to billiards.

Previously the home of the Hunnewell-Shepley family, State Street Mansion was designed in 1805 by Alexander Parris. After purchasing the building in 1922, the Portland Club added a ballroom and commissioned Stevens to modify Parris's arcade. The portico parapet was removed and palladian windows and caps added, while also replacing the original columns.

There are eight antique mahogany tables—six pool and two billiards—on the second floor mixed among the others. Popular for celebrations, gatherings, and contests, the room captures the affluence and elegance of the city's pre-Depression era.

156 State St., 207-956-8943
theportlandclub.org

RACE A BOAT
AT MS HARBORFEST

In mid-August, when the summer sun and harbor water is at its warmest, Casco Bay hosts three days of nautical arm flexing. MS Harborfest's seafaring competitions are designed to excite boaters and landlubbing spectators alike, while raising money to combat multiple sclerosis.

Starting with a welcoming reception and fund-raising auction on Friday, the skippers also meet for a friendly reception (and to size up their competitors). White triangles fill the blue seascape surrounding Portland on Saturday as the sailing regatta dominates the day. But Sunday is all about power!

Sunday's quiet is shattered when high-powered engines of lobster boats and tugboats roar at the mouth of the Fore River. Smaller crafts create a waterway drag strip for lobster boats to cut through the harbor for bragging rights.

The tugboat muster finds the workhorses gathering from around the state for a noble nod of mutual respect in a procession in the harbor before attempting to outgun each other in speed races and nose-to-nose pushing duels.

Experiencing this diverse waterfront community join together to raise money to combat multiple sclerosis, a degenerative neurological disease, is reason enough to be here.

eventmam.nationalmssociety.org/harborfest

DECK THE HULLS
IN THE PARADE OF LIGHTS

Hang the lights, illuminate the decorations, blast the music and start the engine for the annual Parade of Lights in Portland Harbor. Festively lit vessels of all classes, shapes, and sizes join a procession looping around Portland Harbor every second Saturday in December.

Led by tugboats, sailboats, yachts, small power boats, and Casco Bay Line ferries loaded with landlubbers circle from the harbor island to the Casco Bay Bridge. Tugboat captains become nautical ballerinas, spinning tugs while maintaining course during the procession. Fireworks shoot off a waterfront pier and boats to the delight of shoreline spectators, signaling the finale.

If you don't have your own boat, hop aboard Casco Bay Line ferries. One ship has a full bar on board, the other does not...but that vessel is BYOB!

Ticket sales benefit the SailMaine program. This nonprofit helps underprivileged children in this seaport city learn how to harness the power of wind and experience the joys of sailing.

56 Commercial St., 207-774-7871
cascobaylines.com

ICE SKATE
IN DEERING OAKS PARK

When the wind blows cold, the skates come out! Portland is one of the great remaining cities that embraces ice skating in its city park. The picturesque pond, fronted by an adorable 1894 Frederick Thompson stone castle, was once connected to the tidal basin of Portland's Back Cove. The pond has provided free skating to residents for more than a couple of centuries, and figure skaters and hockey players still hit the ice at all hours.

The setting is so magical that a romantic skating scene was filmed with Denzel Washington playing an angel who falls for Whitney Houston in *The Preacher's Wife* (1996). Envisioned by the Olmsted Company, it's not surprising that Deering Oaks and its pond—reminiscent of the landscape design company's other park projects in New York City—served as a stand-in for the Big Apple setting.

Deering Oaks Park pond
207-756-8275
deeringoaks.org

TIP
Bring your skates, as there are none to rent. Also, check the castle hours with the city if you want to warm up . . . or use its indoor bathrooms when you go.

SKI THE STREETS
OF PORTLAND

Noted by *USA Today* as one of the top urban cities for cross-country skiing in the United States, it is not uncommon to see locals gliding down Exchange Street, enjoying a full-body cardio commute after a snowy nor'easter.

A few inches of powder over Old Port cobblestones create scenic city byways for Nordic urbanites happy to hit the snow from their door. But even if the snowplows restore traffic before you're ready to return, Portland Trails's interconnected web of paths runs parallel with city streets and waterfront vistas, offering visual distractions on the way home.

Anywhere in Portland

IF THE STREETS ARE PLOWED, OTHER POPULAR SPOTS INCLUDE:
All of Portland Trails • Eastern Promenade • Western Promenade • Evergreen Cemetery • Deering Oaks Park • Payson Park • Baxter Woods • Mackworth Island • Riverside Golf Course

If you want the workout but prefer walking, snowshoeing is a popular alternative.

FINISH
THE MAINE MARATHON

"People who don't run the Maine Marathon are missing something fun . . . especially when the knees go out at mile sixteen," laughs runner Laura Peterson. "I didn't care if I crawled—I was crossing that finish line."

The sense of accomplishment is only part of the drive to run early October's twenty-six-mile race—it also traverses some of the loveliest byways in the region. Starting with a deceptively easy two miles around the western side of Portland's Back Cove, the course heads north on Route 1 across Casco Bay into Falmouth. Runners bear right up Route 88, beginning the hills on this Foreside Road through Cumberland. The journey continues to the turnaround at Yarmouth's Prince's Point.

The return retraces the hills along the leafy mansion-lined road back to Portland. Energy from the community bolsters runners, with residents cheering the competitors in the suburban towns. Back in Portland, runners pick up the Back Cove trail again through Payson Park for the home stretch. The finish in Portland is "family friendly," Peterson says. "Our kids are able to come out at the end and run across the finish line with us." Props are given to first-time marathoners as finishing times are announced to the crowd.

Start at Baxter Blvd. near Preble St., 207-749-9160
mainemarathon.com

CELEBRITY WATCH
IN THE OLD PORT

Portland's world-class recording studio, scenic locales, burgeoning culinary reputation, and home-grown talent seem to be attracting more celebrities to Portland. Sit back and enjoy the show.

Lady Gaga, Billy Joel, Eric Clapton, and other recording artists frequent the waterfront while in town recording with Bob Ludwig's Grammy-Award-winning Gateway Mastering.

Leonardo DiCaprio has been spotted dodging recognition at The Portland Harbor Hotel, a pregnant Julia Roberts famously lived at what is now the Westin Portland Harborview while her husband filmed a movie. The Press Hotel is a frequent stop for performers headlining at Merrill Auditorium across the street.

Kirsten Dunst has dined at Fore Street restaurant. Rob Morrow sang for his supper at The Porthole. Alton Brown tweets his love of Vena's Fizz House to the world, Adam Richman, Anthony Bourdain, Eric Ripert, and various TV-food show celebrities keep returning to this culinary destination.

It's not unusual to spot Anna Kendrick, Patrick Dempsey, Liv Tyler, Judd Nelson, Linda Lavin, Andrea Martin, Christopher Fitzgerald, Victoria Rowell, "Survivor Bob" Crowley, and Robert Plant in town while visiting relatives over holidays and vacations.

Anywhere in the Old Port, with emphasis on Tommy's Park, Long Wharf, Exchange Street, and area restaurants.

BASKETBALL FINALS
AT THE CROSS INSURANCE ARENA

It's not March Madness, but it's close—literally! The last week in February and first weekend in March, the deciding games of the state final basketball championship are played in Portland. It may not be the collegiate rivalries facing off the following month, but you'd never know it by the deafening chants coming from the Spring Street stadium when the two top high school teams in their class reach the hardwood.

One of Portland's high schools often makes the cut. If a hometown team takes the floor, you may need earplugs. If two city-based schools face off, earplugs won't help. When Deering High School (est. 1874) won its first state championship in 2012, it may as well have been the NBA finals at Boston Garden.

You don't need to like basketball to enjoy the enthusiasm and passion of the crowd at a live championship game, but it's wise to not wear one team's colors on the other team's side of the stadium seating—even accidentally!

1 Civic Center Square, 207-775-3458
crossarenaportland.com

CHEER LIKE A LOCAL (AND WEAR THE COLORS)
Portland Bulldogs: blue & white, bark a lot. • Deering Rams: purple & white • Cheverus Stags: purple & gold • Maine Girls' Academy Lady Lions: green & gold • Waynflete Flyers: green & white

RAPPEL A HIGHRISE
FOR RIPPLEFFECT

"I am deathly afraid of heights, and then you hear those two words that fill my heart with [dread]: 'Lean back!' It is the most unnatural feeling!" says Jack Lufkin about his experience descending from one of the tallest buildings in Portland. "But the confidence as the ropes have you makes this such an appropriate experience for the effect Rippleffect has on these kids."

The 150-foot drop in Canal Plaza, normally associated with rural cliffs, is open to one hundred folks looking for an urban adventure. The opportunity to abseil is afforded to those who secure $500 or more in fundraising for Rippleffect, a nonprofit supporting youth development and leadership, largely through kayak-related programs. The two-day event in mid-May raises $40,000, supporting Rippleffect's scholarship, education, and leadership efforts.

The event's safety is ensured with Over the Edge's supervision, a rappelling-event company with skilled professionals and state-of-the-art equipment. With nothing below to break the fall, the equipment won't let you descend quickly, even if you want to. First-time rappellers can hone their skills beforehand on smaller buildings or parking garages nearby. And the Liquid Courage cocktail reception Friday night will help get participants over the edge. Eyes closed the whole way down? A helmet cam will preserve the memory and even capture digital stills. Scream away.

1 City Center, 207-791-7870
rappelforripple.net

WHALE OF A TAIL
ON ODYSSEY WHALE WATCH

After seeing a whale breach for the first time, the drama and wonder of Herman Melville's *Moby Dick* takes on a whole new dimension. Odyssey Whale Watch tours depart Long Wharf from spring through late fall in search of the migrating undersea behemoths. While catching sight of humpbacks, finbacks, or minke whales is likely, it's not unheard of to also see sharks, North Atlantic white-sided dolphins, and sea turtles, as numerous species of seabirds escort the ship anticipating a free meal.

There are more tours in the warmer months when the daylight is longer, but the single-voyage months of spring and autumn are when whales migrate, so odds are better for multiple sightings along the way. The crew works closely with other marine professionals tracking the large mammals to set a course to meet them along their journey.

170 Commercial St., 207-775-0727
odysseywhalewatch.com

TIP
As warm as it may be on shore, it can be as much as ten to twenty degrees cooler on the open North Atlantic, so bring layers. If you're a flatlander or landlubber, or just prone to motion sickness, bring Dramamine . . . the trip over the ocean swells can be a four-hour roller-coaster ride at times.

IT MAKES A VILLAGE
ON MACKWORTH ISLAND

On the lee side of Mackworth Island is a clearing where natural elements from the surrounding woods create structures for the tiny fairies who inhabit the island. Inventive homes, stores, apartment complexes, and even an airport (fairies have to land somewhere) have popped up over the years. All the architectural acumen is useless without a good contractor, so children visiting the island construct the buildings with skillfully arranged twigs, leaves, branches, rocks, and whatever is found. Material foreign to the island is not allowed for ecological reasons.

Over the years the village has become more of a fairy city. It suffers from urban sprawl like so many popular areas impacted by overbuilding. But so many children know that if you build it, they will come, and everyone knows you can't have enough fairies around.

Island access off Route 1 at end of Andrews Ave.
Falmouth
trails.org/our-trails/mackworth-island-trail

TIP
Governor Percival P. Baxter deeded Calendar Island bordering Portland to create the Governor Baxter School for the Deaf. The deed required that the island always remain accessible to the public for recreation. Additionally, he included a provision ensuring that his pet cemetery with his beloved Irish setters and a horse also be preserved. Since then, the perimeter of the hundred-acre island is regularly trodden by thousands of people, many of whom come to house the fairies.

CATCH YOUR BREATH
AT STANDPIPE PARK

It's hard to catch your breath at a place that takes your breath away, but do try and absorb the city panorama from this North Street park. Standpipe Park hides in plain sight. No one seems to know it by one name. It's called North Street Park, Fort Sumner Park after the World War II military installation on the site, Shailer Park after the adjacent former school building, or "oh, there!" This patch of grass owns one of the most picturesque precipices east of San Francisco's Pacific Heights.

From the ridge looking right, a glimpse of the blue harbor can be seen through downtown financial center high-rises pierced by the Cathedral of the Immaculate Conception's spires. Carrère and Hastings's distinctive city hall tower is almost blocked by Franklin Towers (Maine's tallest building). Further right, the Westin Portland Harborview seems almost the same height as Maine Medical Center's hilltop elevation. From there, the peninsula slopes down into the gentrifying Bayside neighborhood, where industrial brick warehouses and scrapyards are intermixed with coffee houses, breweries, and chain stores. Sleek towers suddenly pop up next to Back Cove's field of dazzling blue water. The oval outlined with emerald trees fades into the wavy horizon of the White Mountains to the west.

It's a calming portrait of Maine's largest city.

60 North St.

OTHER NOTABLE PUBLIC-SPACE VIEWS IN PORTLAND

Casco Bay Bridge
Seagull's-eye views of the harbor and city will surprise.

Baxter Boulevard & Payson Park
Skyline across Back Cove

Western Promenade
Sunset over the New Hampshire mountains

Eastern Promenade
Over Portland Harbor looking "down bay"

CIRCLE AROUND
BACK COVE

Most days, hundreds of urban dwellers (and four-legged companions) circle the tidal basin below the western slope of Portland's downtown. The Back Cove is surrounded by trails, paved roads, and athletic fields to unwind or enjoy nature. The three-and-a-half-mile loop is often used as a training course for 5K races and marathons, but it's also enjoyed for an easy stroll.

The body of water is a picturesque recreational backdrop for runners, power walkers, bicyclists, and—in winter—cross-country skiers. Anchored by two large parking lots at opposite ends, starting points can either be close to downtown in the shadow of the Intermed skyscraper or in the East Deering neighborhood's pastoral Payson Park.

Along the way, wildlife, flora and fauna, grand homes, and the city skyline are on hand to visually distract from "feeling the burn." Elegant double bridges were constructed in the early 1920s, and their now-consolidated waterside respite is still a picturesque half-way point. Rest or just take in the city.

If the route seems too short, Back Cove Trail connects into the seventy-mile labyrinth of Portland Trails.

trails.org/our-trails/back-cove-trail

POLAR BEAR DIP & DASH
OFF EAST END BEACH

A collective shriek of shock and awe breaks the New Year's Eve quiet as a giant polar bear (okay, person in a polar bear costume) urges hundreds of people into frigid Atlantic waters at noon the last day of each year. It's the Natural Resources Council of Maine's annual fund-raiser, where people who are environmentally conscious, checking off a bucket list item, or have lost a bet, plunge into ocean water averaging thirty-seven degrees to bring awareness to global climate change and its effect on Maine.

Their dashing back onto the sand into warm towels held by friends, family, and supporters is not, however, the reason for the name. Those looking for a warm-up run beforehand can dash in a 5K race at 11 a.m. around the nearby Back Cove Trail. Shuttle buses deliver them to East End Beach for the noontime dip.

East End Beach is on the base of the Eastern Promenade and has the distinction of being the only beach in the city. The Munjoy Hill neighborhood location is convenient for attracting participants, and picturesque views of the Calendar Islands and harbor forts allow them to focus on anything else as they hit the water running.

No matter your scientific or political beliefs, a fun time is had by all . . . and the water's still friggin' cold!

East End Beach
nrcm.kintera.org/dipdash

CAMP OUT
AT FORT GORGES

Fort Gorges is a massive stone military fortress that seems to float in Portland's harbor. Its location is close enough for stunning views of the city skyline, but far enough to see a blanket of stars at night. Once in the hexagonal fort, its seclusion is enough to feel a world away from the nearby urban center . . . perfect for camping!

Built in 1857 and named after Ferdinand Gorges, an original landowner of Portland, the fort is a monument to nineteenth-century military architecture. Now listed on the National Register of Historic Places, the city-owned fort has no public transportation. A perilous approach by private craft requires skilled navigation. Beyond the arched levels, gunnery mounts, and torpedo storehouse, it's discovering the massive ten-inch Parrott gun settled in the grass parapet that excites visitors. The length of several people, the cannon was deemed too large to remove when the fort was decommissioned.

A well-used firepit is safely in the former parade grounds, but it is wise to bring wood as well as any other supplies. There are no trees in the fort, much less electricity, stores, or anything else. It's as close to roughing it as you can get in a city.

Officially a city park, Friends of Fort Gorges are working toward easier public access that may include regular ferry service and evolving it into Portland's ultimate outdoor performance venue.

Hog Island Ledge in Portland Harbor
friendsoffortgorges.org

ROLL YOUR OWN
AT BAYSIDE BOWL

It's clear the retro sign illuminated high above Alder Street promising ten-pin bowling in Portland's industrial Bayside neighborhood is deceptively understated when entering this sleek downtown bowling center.

The creation of Charlie Mitchell and Justin Alfond (favorite sons of political royalty in Maine), was an early entry into the area's gentrification efforts. By more than tripling the alley's original size in expanding a single level warehouse factory building into a premier multi-story venue, Bayside Bowl has become a preferred darling for ESPN and the Professional Bowlers Association (PBA). Capturing the attention of bowlers and fans alike, the venue has become the home of PBA's Elias Cup, featuring superstar bowlers from around the word.

But if rolling turkeys and gutter balls is not your thing, enjoy the great food, live bands, or spectacular views. The original lanes, harvested from a private alley in an area mansion, are in the low-rise brick warehouse with cozy island bar and stage for live performances. The newer side has the PBA-regualtion lanes with gleaming balcony loft and function rooms.

But the crown jewel of Bayside is the solar-paneled roof with expansive 360°-panorama deck, complete with full bar and vintage Airstream trailer serving gourmet tacos.

The Dude abides.

58 Alder St., Portland, 207-791-2695
baysidebowl.com

CULTURE AND HISTORY

BE INSPIRED
AT WINSLOW HOMER'S STUDIO

People are often mesmerized seeing the sea-green waves churning foam as they dramatically crash on the rock-lined edge of Checkly Point. Such is the power of Winslow Homer's art. Many of his paintings in the Portland Museum of Art boldly depict Maine's coast. But Homer's work imitates life—his life—at his studio, now also part of the PMA, which offers guided tours.

A twenty-minute ride from the downtown museum, Homer's studio is in the exclusive enclave of Scarborough's Prouts Neck. After enjoying a decade of summers, the artist sought the peaceful beauty of Maine over Manhattan, hiring noted architect John Calvin Stevens in 1884 to convert a carriage house into a residence. His primary residence until his death in 1910, it's difficult to not feel the inspiration Homer drew from the natural surroundings outside his fifteen-hundred-square-foot studio.

Portland Museum of Art
7 Congress Sq.
(Studio tours are transported only via PMA's museum shuttle
from downtown to 5 Winslow Homer Rd., Scarborough.)
207-775-6148
portlandmuseum.org/homer

GET YOUR GREEK ON
AT THE GREEK FESTIVAL

You don't need a big, fat Greek wedding to be welcomed into a Greek family. Just head to the corner of Park and Pleasant Streets and shout "Opa!" one weekend in June. Laughter and dancing accompany the authentic music, food, and drink of the Mediterranean culture at the annual festival in Portland's West End.

"Any excuse to be Greek!" says Konstantina Rigas. The twenty-five-year-old enjoys embracing her heritage at Maine's largest Greek festival, coming thirty miles to dance and "express my Greekness—I'm all over it!"

Exuberant sounds and scents explode from a normally quiet Holy Trinity Greek Orthodox Church, inviting the world to celebrate. Flash mob Kalamatianós dances continue late into the night around stately Federal brick townhomes, as ouzo-happy revelers spontaneously break into the popular counterclockwise folk dance.

133 Pleasant St., 207-774-0281
holytrinityportland.org

OTHER CULTURAL FESTIVALS
Festival of Nations, Italian Heritage Festival, Southern Maine Pride Parade and Festival

SEE THE LIGHT
ON MAINE OPEN LIGHTHOUSE DAY

Portland Harbor is protected by no fewer than five lighthouses, all within a ten-minute drive of each other (a private craft is required for the sixth). This cluster allows enthusiasts the opportunity to scale almost one-fifth of the state's towers during Maine Open Lighhouse Day. Organized by the Maine Office of Tourism and the American Lighthouse Foundation, cherished beacons normally off limits to the public are accessible during one Saturday each September.

While each of the sentinels in Casco Bay has a unique design and rich history, the one to not miss exploring is Portland Head Light. Commissioned by George Washington, the ninety-foot tower is a must-see. Classic in design and dramatic in setting, it is believed to be the most photographed in the world, sitting on majestic cliffs with crashing waves—right out of film noir.

Whichever you choose to visit, do not be discouraged by bad weather. Lighthouses were built to save ships in blinding seas, so experiencing a sweeping beam cutting through the rain on a stormy night may be the best way to see these beacons in action! And there is no better sound on a misty night than the low moan of a foghorn.

American Lighthouse Foundation, 207-594-4174
lighthousefoundation.org

PORTLAND HARBOR LIGHTHOUSES (BY YEAR BUILT)

1. Portland Head Light, 1791, Cape Elizabeth
2. Two Lights/Cape Elizabeth Light—East, 1874, Cape Elizabeth
3. Two Lights/Cape Elizabeth Light—West, 1874, Cape Elizabeth
4. Portland Breakwater (Bug) Light, 1875, South Portland
5. Spring Point Ledge Light, 1897, South Portland
6. Ram Island Ledge Light, 1905, Ram Island

TIP

Portland Head Light, one of the most popular lights on Maine Lighthouse Day, has limited (free) tickets available on a first come, first served basis, so go early! And you'll still have time for the other lighthouses close by.

STAND ATOP
THE PORTLAND OBSERVATORY

Standing beside Portland Observatory's cupola, visitors are transported to a time before cell phones, walkie-talkies, and radio, when visual signals were the only way to communicate. Technological advances in navigation have rendered observatories obsolete—so much so that Portland's 1807 wood tower is the last of its kind on the entire continent.

During the age of sailing, shipment schedules were little more than a good guess. Ships would sail into port without warning and owners would scramble to find men to off-load the goods, which could take days. Captain Lemuel Moody had experienced this frustration firsthand, and was inspired by the ports of call with signal towers.

Moody constructed his tower at the apex of Munjoy Hill with a telescope capable of seeing a craft up to sixty miles away. Often taken for a lighthouse, Portland Observatory shares a similar design to withstand the same high winds and severe weather at its exposed position.

As visitors soak in the views of Casco Bay, the city skyline, and New Hampshire's White Mountains to the west, it's amazing to know signal towers like this were in far-flung ports, spotting incoming vessels to alert owners that their ship was literally coming in. Dock workers were assembled and waiting when the cargo arrived.

138 Congress St., 207-774-5561
portlandlandmarks.org/observatory

TIP

The Industrial Revolution was not the only threat over the years. Moody's tower was the lone wooden structure to survive the Great Fire of 1866. Tales were related of Moody's workers pouring water down the observatory's sides while the inferno was raging around them. It was the only standing structure in the East End neighborhood after the conflagration.

THE FIRE HORSES
AT PORTLAND FIRE MUSEUM

Nestled in the West End between State and Park streets you can find a living tribute to the first responders throughout Portland's fire-prone past—particularly the Great Fire of 1866—in the Portland Fire Museum. This boutique museum is the retired Engine 4 station house that served downtown. Squeezed in among the antique trucks, wagons, memorials, and vintage equipment are the original horse stalls. While the original equine inhabitants of this house were full-time residents, the two current horses are here part time.

The city's great conflagration destroyed two-thirds of Portland's downtown on July 4 when firecrackers sparked off wood chips at the waterfront. The flames consumed most of the wooden structures in Portland, from the waterfront wharves all the way up through the East End. It remained the worst urban fire until Chicago met Mrs. O'Leary's cow five years later.

The museum began in 1891 when the Portland Veteran Firemen's Association decided to share their memories of battling the blaze with generations to come. The PVFA has grown the collection over the past century.

Inside the granite firehouse, guests learn fire prevention. Explore the horse-driven water wagon, view vintage films featuring the museum when it was an active station, and visit the horses while soaking in the history.

157 Spring St., 207-772-2040
portlandfiremuseum.com

HALLOWEEN PARADE
THROUGH THE WEST END

Ghosts, princesses, goblins, sexy cats, giraffes, witches, superheroes, and politicians are but a few of the characters that join in on the fun of the West End Halloween Parade every October 31.

The neighborhood's parade starts in front of Reiche Community Center on Brackett Street at 6 p.m. and loops though the historic West End. A tradition for more than thirty years, colorful fifteen-foot puppets lead masked marchers of all ages into the neighborhood's winding streets. Along the route, children jump out of the procession in their quest for candy.

The West End Historic District includes many Gothic homes that are listed on the National Register of Historic Places. These Victorian-style mansions enhance the haunted holiday's fun as trick-or-treaters bound up the steps of what could well be the mansions of the Addams Family. Some residents even decorate their carriage houses with creepy themes, creating free interactive haunted houses, which adds a level of excitement and fun for neighborhood children (and adults) as they retrieve their treats.

While the nineteenth-century buildings hardly need decorations, many up the ante in a determined effort to preserve a tradition of door-to-door trick-or-treating in a welcoming community, creating joyful memories for another generation.

Reiche Community Center
166 Brackett St.
Oct. 31, 6 p.m.

VISIT THE BERLIN WALL
ON LONG WHARF

People strolling along Long Wharf are often surprised to discover three panels of cement with faded graffiti from Germany that were once brightly colored depictions celebrating the Communist Party's fall from power in Europe. The most prominent of the whimsical images is of the Soviet hammer-and-sickle logo in flames boasting "The Party's Over!"

A reminder of the recent twenty-fifth anniversary of the eighty-seven-mile wall's destruction, the three panels are an unappreciated treasure on Portland's waterfront. Representing the oppression literally surrounding West Berlin for twenty-eight years, this section is one of only fifty-four in the United States.

Long Wharf near 170 Commercial St.

Also visit the Heroes Wall on Long Wharf and pay respect to the brave members of the military from Maine whose contributions help secure the freedoms the nearby Berlin Wall fragments attempted to repress.

COLONIAL LIFE
IN THE TATE HOUSE MUSEUM

The clapboard home in Stroudwater seems almost unremarkable compared to the large homes surrounding it, but the Tate House predates many of its neighbors by more than a century. The colonial-era home was constructed by Captain George Tate in 1755.

Founded in 1657, Stroudwater Village is situated along the Fore River as it widens into Portland's inner harbor. Captain Tate's home reflected his important role in the British Royal Navy, overseeing production of the ships' masts harvested from Maine's white pines—it's not called the Pine Tree State for nothing. From his prominent Georgian-style home, the captain could monitor progress as trees came downriver for shipment outside–his front porch view of the Fore River serving as the ultimate factory floor. With its subsumed dormer on a gambrel roof, extensive herb garden, and period furniture, the Tate House would have been considered enormous in the colonial era.

With the British Navy's destruction of Portland (then called Falmouth) in 1775, the Tate House Museum is one of the oldest remaining structures in Portland, and the only colonial-era residence open to the public. The eighteenth-century home is a National Historic Landmark.

1267 Westbrook St., 207-774-6177
tatehouse.org

SEE, PRAY, LOVE
AT THE MAINE JEWISH MUSEUM

"Exhibits are by contemporary artists who must have a Jewish connection and a Maine connection," says Maine Jewish Museum curator Nancy Davidson. The museum is part of a still-active synagogue downtown. "Every two months we rotate shows." But the art isn't the only attraction. Stained glass windows in the simple brick edifice hint at architectural treasure inside. The sanctuary awes with "modest grandeur," boasting a domed ceiling and elegant woodwork familiar in houses of worship from the era.

The building was restored as an "unaffiliated synagogue— everyone is welcome!" explains Davidson. "The first floor is for shows and Orthodox services, and the sanctuary on the second floor is active and used for Reform services." A third floor highlights original Jewish residents in Maine and their contributions. Occasional high-profile touring shows are also presented.

Formerly an apartment building, Etz Chaim ("Tree of Life") Synagogue was converted in 1921 by a congregation without a temple. The Tree of Life organization was formed and ensures Etz Chaim remains one of "the oldest European-style synagogues in continuous use in Maine."

267 Congress St., 207-773-2339
mainejewishmuseum.org

HUNT BEARS
ON THE LANGLAIS ART TRAIL

At Ocean Gateway, visitors are greeted by an amusingly ferocious Standing Bear (1977) towering fifteen feet, while two Playing Bears (1976–77) sit by the grand staircase in Portland International Jetport. These are two examples of legacy artist Bernard "Blackie" Langlais.

Langlais's sculptures numbered in the thousands when he died in 1977. A small portion of his massive body of work is displayed throughout the city. His wood sculptures were gifted to Portland by Colby College and Kohler Foundation Inc. for display around the city as part of the state's Langlais Art Trail. His larger-than-life bear sculptures are hiding in plain sight, surprising visitors and locals alike.

langlaisarttrail.org

LANGLAIS ART TRAIL IN PORTLAND

Deering High School
Untitled, 1976 –77, wood, paint, and nails; wood and
paint, 36 × 20 × 17 in.; 37 × 16 × 15 in. Portland
Public Art Committee, gift of Colby College and
Kohler Foundation Inc. (two heads)

Portland High School
Untitled, 1977, wood and paint, 26.5 in.; 26.5 in.;
33.5 in. Portland Public Art Committee, gift of Colby
College and Kohler Foundation Inc.
(three heads—the high school rivalry continues . . .)

University of New England Gallery of Art
Untitled, wood on wood, 64.5 × 29.25 × 3.5 in.
University of New England Art Gallery,
gift of Colby College and Kohler Foundation Inc.
(looks kind of like an abstract lobster)

Portland Museum of Art
Noon Exercise, 1963, pine, 116 × 88.5 in. Portland
Museum of Art, purchased with support from the
Robert R. Masterton Memorial Fund and Helen
Langlais. (prancing horse)

Portland Public Library—Main Branch
Elephant, 1976 –77, wood. Portland Public Art
Committee, gift of Colby College and Kohler
Foundation Inc.

BACH & ROLL
AT THE VIRTUOSI FESTIVAL

"It has always been about the music!" says Lewis Kaplan, Director of the Bach Virtuosi Festival. "I had a vision to bring the greatest baroque artists to Portland to perform the music of Johann Sebastian Bach in intimate venues."

Kaplan presents this classical concert series performed by world-renowned musicians over two weekends in mid-June. Concert venues are selected for their intimate feel and exceptional acoustics. The goal is for the audience to be close to the music and add a level of appreciation for Bach's exalted music.

Indeed, *literally* feeling the music emanate from the instruments within feet of you is overwhelming enough, but within the elegant surroundings, including Portland's St. Luke's Cathedral and Etz Chaim Synagogue downtown with vaulted ceilings and glowing stained glass, the experience becomes postively surreal.

As Senior Professor of Violin and Chamber Music at The Juilliard School, Kaplan has extraordinary insight into how to pair the perfect venue with Bach's vision, and engage a twenty-first century audience with the baroque repertoire.

Kaplan assures, "Portland will once again have world class performances of Bach played with both brilliance and love."

bachvirtuosifestival.org

SING IN THE RAIN
AT THE UMBRELLA COVER MUSEUM

An exuberant accordion-wielding woman startles guests walking in this tiny Peaks Island museum, ready to pepper unsuspecting visitors about the wonders of the umbrella cover—that's right, no umbrellas, just the forgotten protective sheaths. If it looks uncomfortably like a room full of used prophylactics, she can show you the "X-rated umbrella cover room," which is (happily) a bit of an overstatement.

Founding director and curator Nancy 3. Hoffman (not a misprint—her middle name is legally "3") started her collection innocently enough. Discovering half a dozen umbrella covers, she didn't know what to do with them. A museum was born. Years ago, Guinness World Records recognized her cover inventory as the largest at 730, even though the covers now top 1,200. Would anyone else admit to having more? Hoffman hopes not! Her enthusiasm and energy is contagious.

"More people [find us], and every season gets better and better," she says. "The international press went bonkers."

Hoffman challenges visitors with jokes and contests that cannot be refused. But that doesn't hold a candle to her talent on the piano accordion. She seems to have a tune for everything and is ready to play at the drop of a hat. She sings songs in twenty-one languages (she only speaks four).

62-B Island Ave., Peaks Island, 207-939-0301
umbrellacovermuseum.org

NEW YEAR'S EVE
AT THE VICTORIA MANSION

Traditional tuxedos and high-contrast dresses—some with white gloves—give life to the Victoria Mansion's Black & White Soiree. On the last night of the year, the formal fête welcomes midnight in a way Jay Gatsby would envy. Portland's Gaslight League hosts parties to complement the opulent Morse-Libby House (named after the two families that owned it) with over-the-top holiday cheer. The museum home, already decorated with period-appropriate extravagance for Christmas, is enlivened with the group's Roaring Twenties New Year's celebration.

"It's so opulent, you can't ever overdo it," says Dan Kennedy, owner of Harmon's & Barton's florist, who has contributed to the holiday decor since 1991. "I've developed a passion for decorating it."

The inspiration of development director Sam Heck, the self-described social club's membership consists of a "diverse and creative group of cocktail enthusiasts, partygoers, and history buffs."

The Gaslight League also parties with a hearty Mardi Gras Fête on Fat Tuesday (an obvious fit considering the New Orleans connection), a Steampunk Masquerade on Halloween, and a summer soiree.

109 Danforth St., 207-772-4841
victoriamansion.org

TIP

The home is open for public tours May-January, so the home, including Christmas decor, can be enjoyed regardless of Prohibition. Those who prefer a nightmare before Christmas can be enveloped in Victoria Mansion's Tales of Terror during Halloween. This, however, is no carnival haunted house. While creepy-looking folks may greet you, it is an evening of theatrical readings. If that doesn't sound frightening, then you've never heard Edgar Allan Poe done right. And, really, doesn't everyone dressed in Victorian-era clothing look like they could be Jack the Ripper?

• •

HISTORY

Ironically, the majestic brownstone was constructed for Ruggles Sylvester Morse as a summer home and would have never been inhabited during the winter holidays. The Portland native and New Orleans hotelier had the brownstone townhouse built (1858–1863) to escape the southern heat. Stuck below the Mason-Dixon line through the Civil War, he was unable to enjoy his new Italianate villa–style getaway for almost four years.

Joseph Ralph Libby bought the mansion, but made no significant alterations. Abandoned during the Great Depression, the landmark escaped demolition, and the museum was created in 1941. The Libby heirs donated furnishings the family had kept— more than ninety percent—making the Victoria Mansion a veritable time capsule.

SUNRISE SERVICE
AT FORT ALLEN PARK

If sitting in a crowded church being hit by oversized bonnets isn't for you, join other faithful followers at Fort Allen's gazebo and be one of the first in the United States to welcome the Easter morning sun. The pre-dawn gathering is informal and casual. Fleece coats and L.L. Bean boots are more likely to be worn than silk dresses and high heels when people gather on the circular bandstand waiting for the sun.

All faiths are welcome to join. The Stevens Avenue Congregational Church doesn't discriminate . . . especially on Easter morning. Part of the United Church of Christ (UCC) denomination, the parish has deep religious roots in colonial New England Puritanism, but the modern-day church encourages interfaith celebration and inclusion. Strangers are welcomed as warmly as the congregation.

When the ocean begins to reflect the red streaks in the glowing sky, the people circle around to reflect on the day. Fort Allen's perch at the end of the Eastern Promenade hovers above the channel to the open bay, affording expansive views over Portland Harbor. The deep blue sky changes from red to orange, and then eases into a hot yellow as bright rays crest the Atlantic. The sun's climb over the ocean softens the brightening sky, sending sparkles across the waves below. Commuter ferries from Peaks Island glint in the morning sun as they pass by Fort Gorges.

Fort Allen Park Gazebo
207-797-4573

TIP

Easter dates differ every year, so
the time of sunrise services changes.
Services are rain or shine, because the
assumption is that the sun is shining
somewhere, so regardless,
"He is risen, indeed."

RAINY DAY ROOM
AT WADSWORTH-LONGFELLOW HOUSE & GARDEN

Most people know the phrase, "Into each life some rain must fall" by Henry Wadsworth Longfellow, but few know where it was created. His 1841 poem "The Rainy Day" was composed in a room that overlooked the garden in the back of the family home. The desk on which he penned the poem still stands sentry. The Colonial Revival–style gardens in the back of the house are original, including an eighteenth-century lilac planting Longfellow may have cared for himself. It's open as a public respite amid the tall downtown buildings.

Some are under the misguided impression that the literary giant is from Boston, but his childhood home fronts Congress Street in Portland's center city. Built by his grandfather, General Peleg Wadsworth, in 1786, the home remained in the family until Henry's sister, Anne, bequeathed it in 1901 as a museum, understanding her brother's profound impact on the world.

489 Congress St., 207-774-1822
mainehistory.org/house_overview.shtml

Henry's sister, Anne Longfellow Pierce, ensured the family estate remained as it was when her brother spent his childhood there. She decided to preserve the home long before she passed away to honor his memory for future generations. This extended to never installing plumbing in the house. Throughout her life, until she died at age ninety-one in 1901, she resolutely crossed the street to city hall and renewed her privy license.

PAY YOUR RESPECTS
IN THE EASTERN CEMETERY

Portland's oldest public burial grounds is the Eastern Cemetery at the base of Munjoy Hill. As a colonial-era cemetery, it's on the National Register of Historic Places. With over thirty-five hundred recorded deceased, interments ceased during the Civil War.

The five-acre field has ornately carved headstones (and footstones). These memorials are impressive for their artistry as much as their history. A distinctive tombstone in the northwest corner with a carved soldier's bedroll marks the grave of Alonzo P. Stinson, who died fighting in the First Battle of Bull Run. He is the first Portlander known to be killed in the War between the States.

Other grave markers include two enemy ship captains, both mortally wounded in an epic sea battle during the War of 1812. British Captain Samuel Blythe surrendered the HMS *Boxer* to American Lieutenant William Ward Burrows II of the USS *Enterprise*, deciding the sea battle off the Maine coast before both masters died of their injuries. Ironically, they lie side-by-side forever in the rear of the graveyard. Fascination with their graves as a boy inspired local bar owner Josh Miranda to open Blyth & Burrows bar in the Old Port (complete with speakeasy Broken Dram behind the bookcase in the rear alley).

224 Congress St.
spiritsalive.org

TIP

Eastern Cemetery is accessible even when locked. Visitors who want to pay respects when gates are closed only need cross the street to get the key from a local merchant—appropriately, vintage book dealer Carlson & Turner Antiquarian Books is the keeper of the keys. Otherwise, make arrangements with Spirits Alive, the volunteer organization that maintains the historic hallowed ground, keeping it open for the public.

241 Congress St., 207-773-4200
carlsonturnerbooks.com

OTHER PORTLAND CEMETERIES

Evergreen Cemetery, Deering Center
First Parish Church, Intown
Western Cemetery, West End

STAND NEXT TO BIGFOOT
AT THE INTERNATIONAL CRYPTOZOOLOGY MUSEUM

Loren Coleman claims that his collection of paraphernalia attributed to oddities, legends, and folklore is "the world's only cryptozoology museum," and that may very well be true. Where else could one see an "authentic fake" Feejee Mermaid? No, not Fiji. The film prop from P.T. Barnum is one of many artifacts and souvenirs exhibited.

Small in size, it's big in feet—the collection includes one hundred creatures' foot casts from sightings worldwide, and the museum's signature attraction and most popular photo op is an eight-foot-tall Bigfoot. The museum includes additional TV and film pieces, as well as the original artifact that started it all for Coleman: the burgee flag from the World Book's Snowman Expedition to the Himalayas led by Edmund Hillary and Marlin Perkins. Founded in 2003, the museum started in Coleman's private home and grew into its current downtown location just off Congress Street.

Founded in 2003, the museum went from Coleman's private home and grew into its current Thompson's Point location. Whether its public fascination with the unexplained, because of *Time* magazine's listing it as one of the "Ten Weirdest Museums in the World," or Yankee magazine's pick as one of the top five "Kid-Friendly Museums in New England," the museum is getting discovered, to the point of hosting the only International Cryptozoology Conference in Septembers.

4 Thompson's Point Rd., #106, cryptozoologymuseum.com

CAMERA OBSCURA
AT THE CHILDREN'S MUSEUM & THEATRE

A pinpoint of light pierces the darkness in blackened room and suddenly visitors gasp as the walls glow with the city skyline. Cars and people bustling through the streets suddenly splash across the room as the Camera Obscura (latin for "Dark Room") uses the ingenious old-school technology of Leonardo Da Vinci to dazzle Chilren and adults alike.

Another slightly more advanced Camera Obscura focuses a sweeping view of the harbor on a round table-top plane so visitors can gather around to spot their favorite landmarks.

While the concept was studied for centuries, it was Da Vinci whose fascisnation with human optics made the connection of the "Dark Room" optical effects with the human eye as early as 1502. His low-tech creation led to telescopes and cameras.

Located in the Arts District of downtown Portland, the Children's Museum & Theatre of Maine features a wide variety of interactive exhibits and activities for children and families! Fly a space shuttle, spin the world, visit foreign countries and learn about other cultures, pet a starfish, climb a rock wall, fight a fire, captain a pirate ship or lobster boat, or just play in a treehouse. Beyond that, the theatre presents live performances for children, with children, by children! And acting, audition, and improv classes are offered free of charge on scheduled days.

142 Free St., 207-828-1234
kitetails.org

PROHIBITION BIRTHPLACE
AT THE NEAL S. DOW MEMORIAL

Neal S. Dow was mayor of Portland, abolitionist, Civil War hero, and presidential candidate, but he is best known as the father of Prohibition. His Federal-style home tells all the tales.

While the Eighteenth Amendment prohibited the manufacture and sale of alcohol in the United States in 1919, this mayor of Portland secured statewide prohibition in 1851. This pioneering legislation became known as the Maine Law.

Founder of the Temperance Movement, his 1830 West End house is owned by the Maine Woman's Christian Temperance Union. By today's standards, Dow's amassed material is worthy of a *Hoarders* episode, but in a pre-digital age, it is a compelling and comprehensive record of a storied life. His furniture, books, papers, and even death mask—a three-dimensional cast of his face upon his demise—are available for viewing.

The Neal S. Dow Memorial estimates that there were "approximately three hundred establishments selling . . . alcoholic beverages along the roughly one-mile stretch of Portland's major business district . . . during the first half of the 19th century." Oh, if only he could see it now!

714 Congress St., 207-773-7773
nealdowmemorial.org

PORTLAND RUM RIOTS

However sincere Neal S. Dow's motivations may have been, they were undermined by the Portland Rum Riots in 1855.

Dow attributed the rise in drunkenness to the Irish-immigrant seaport workers. The mayor's campaign was less xenophobic and more sociological. His papers and records relate how he was impacted by accounts of alcohol-related abuses and poverty he witnessed in Portland families.

An opposition political party discovered Dow's supply of alcohol stored for medicinal purposes. On the second anniversary of the Maine Law, tensions came to a head. Stirred up over the mayor's apparent hypocrisy, foreign-born citizens stormed city hall. Dow ordered the militia to fire into the mob, killing and wounding several people.

Found not guilty of violating his own law, his reputation was forever damaged politically, and he lost his bid for governor.

THE (OTHER) *MONA LISA*
AT PORTLAND MUSEUM OF ART

"If you went to Paris right now, you'd see the same thing," says Portland Museum of Art's Kristen Levesque of *La Gioconda*, a *Mona Lisa* look-alike in the permanent collection. "It's been sent to Harvard's Straus Center for Conservation and Technical Studies for verification—painted in the same time period (before 1510) by a left-handed painter . . . just no signature to prove it!"

Indeed, Leonardo da Vinci's early-sixteenth-century portrait of a conspiratorial Lisa del Giocondo is the thing that dreams are made of. Like its autographed counterpart hanging in the Louvre since 1797, the PMA's Renaissance painting is also surprisingly small, measuring 64 cm by 54 cm (the *Mona Lisa* is 77 cm by 53 cm). Donated in 1983 by Prouts Neck resident Henry H. Reichhold, the unsigned *La Gioconda* doesn't often see the light of day. Due to its age and potential worth, the painting spends much of its time in the safety of the archives.

Unlike its Parisian doppelgänger, this *Da Vinci Code* goddess will be more approachable with shorter lines. Coming off its first major renovation in thirty years, the PMA has reintroduced this Italian dream girl to her fans for a prolonged appearance in the gallery. If not exhibited, viewings may be scheduled through requests in an Art Study Room.

7 Congress Sq., 207-775-6148
portlandmuseum.org

CONSPIRACY THEORISTS TAKE NOTE

Eerily, like Dan Brown's tale of intrigue, which involves da Vinci's famous *Mona Lisa* and the new I.M. Pei–designed wing of the Louvre Museum in Paris, *La Gioconda* in Portland is exhibited in an art museum with a contemporary addition also designed by Pei. Both paintings are in cities where French culture and art flourished. And Brown's fictional hero-expert is a professor at nearby Harvard, where the Portland painting has been authenticated. Coincidence?

It's no coincidence that the last time the painting was displayed for public viewing, *The Da Vinci Code* had just been released in theaters. The question is, was it an inspired marketing ploy or a calculated diversion? As Brown writes, "So dark the con of man."

• •

Each month, the PMA is open late for cocktails on the third Thursday, and for free on the first Friday. At both events the museum's galleries are accessible for viewing, including the *Mona Lisa* twin if on public display.

PORTLAND UNCHAINED
ON THE FREEDOM TRAIL

First, Portland's Freedom Trail has no relation to Boston's colonial-era struggle for freedom for the United States. The Forest City's trail exposes significant places that aided African Americans' freedom from within the United States. Currently, Maine Freedom Trails, Inc., maps thirteen marked sites "of sixteen that will constitute a permanent walking trail highlighting the people, places, events, and daily life associated with the Underground Railroad and anti-slavery movement in Portland."

The seaport's involvement with the Triangular Trade created conflicted sentiments in this northern state born from the Missouri Compromise. Sites include safe houses owned by active abolitionists; venues that hosted notable figures such as Susan B. Anthony, William Lloyd Garrison, and Frederick Douglass; locations of pro-slavery riots; and other significant links breaking the chains of slavery.

Given the period of the abolitionist movement, it's not surprising that most of the markers are congregated in the Old Port. Still, some markers seem to be missing. One notable absence is abolitionist Neal S. Dow's West End home—a known station on the Underground Railroad. In the party of President Abraham Lincoln, a missing link recognizing the Republican mayor's home is odd.

Beginning at the floor of Franklin St., 207-591-9980

PORTLAND FREEDOM TRAIL SITES

1. Franklin Street Wharf, Casco Bay Lines
2. Barber Shop of Jacob C. Dickson, 243 Fore St.
3. Hack Stand of Charles H. L. Pierre, 29 Middle St.
4. Abyssinian Meeting House, 73 Newbury St.
5. Home of Charles Frederick, Harriet Stephenson Eastman, and Alexander Stephenson, corner of Mountfort and Newbury streets
6. Eastern Cemetery, corner of Congress and Mountfort streets
7. Home of Elias and Elizabeth Widgery Thomas, corner of India and Congress streets
8. Home of General Samuel C. Fessenden, 31 India St.
9. Friends (Quaker) Meeting House, Lincoln Park, corner of Federal and Pearl streets
10. Hack Stand of Reuben Ruby, corner of Federal and Temple streets
11. First Parish Unitarian Universalist Church, 425 Congress St.
12. Secondhand Clothing Store of Lloyd Scott, 44 Exchange St.
13. Mariners' Church, Corner of Fore and Market streets

HOME STREET ADVANTAGE
ON BOWDOIN STREET

Turn-of-the-century architect John Calvin Stevens developed architectural styles in Portland as influential as his midwestern contemporary Frank Lloyd Wright. Inspired by New England- and Victorian-style buildings, Stevens pioneered the Shingle and Colonial Revival styles that quickly swept the Northeast. While Stevens is credited with more than a thousand buildings in Maine, Bowdoin Street off the Western Promenade presents a cluster of his best work, including his own 1882 self-designed home at number 52.

"In time, Bowdoin Street became itself a monument to Stevens and his architectural style," writes John F. Bauman in *Gateway to Vacationland: The Making of Portland, Maine*. Indeed, the short Bowdoin Street is a love letter to Stevens, or rather, a collection of his affectionate missives to Portland. Made with wood, brick, and stone, the houses vary in style as much as they do materials. While his Shingle style is well represented on Bowdoin Street, Stevens's Colonial Revival brick mansion built for lawyer Richard Webb in 1907 at the corner of Vaughan Street anchors the architect's presence.

If the West End street whets the architectural appetite for John Calvin Stevens, there are almost three hundred more buildings to see scattered throughout the city. Another option is to go to the waterfront offices of SMRT—the firm he founded—and hire his great-grandson Paul to design one.

Spans between Western Promenade and Neal St.
portlandlandmarks.org

• •

JOHN CALVIN STEVENS BOWDOIN STREET HOMES

6 Bowdoin St., Richard Edward H. Davies House, 1890

9 Bowdoin St., Nathan Clifford House, 1902; alterations for William M. Bradley, 1906

28 Bowdoin St., Franklin C. Pyson House, 1901

29 Bowdoin St., Richard Webb House, 1907

36 Bowdoin St., Henry L. Houghton House, 1887

40 Bowdoin St., Lucius M. Clark House, 1887–88

41 Bowdoin St., Charles D. Alexander Garage, 1917

44 Bowdoin St., Montgomery S. Hibson House, 1885–86

52 Bowdoin St., John Calvin Stevens House, 1882

55 Bowdoin St., Harrison J. Holt House, 1911

56 Bowdoin St., William H. Dennett House, 1884

62 Bowdoin St., John H. Davis House, 1883

71 Bowdoin St., Herbert Payson House, 1906–7

Information compiled from: *John Calvin Stevens on the Portland Peninsula, 1880 to 1940*, by Earle G. Shettleworth Jr., and https://pinterest.com/mainehistory/john-calvin-stevens

SHOPPING AND FASHION

DRINK 'TIL YOU SHOP
AT MERRY MADNESS

Give in to the (Merry) Madness and eat, drink, and shop downtown all night long on the second Thursday of December. The evening kicks off with a beer and wine red-carpet reception at a downtown venue (alternating annually) at 4 p.m. where revelers pay $15 ($20 at the door) to get in the holiday spirit. The crowd is greeted with delicious bites from local eateries; live music; silent auctions; and a shopping bag with snacks and a commemorative glass filled with a pour of wine, beer, or coffee.

From there, festive holiday shoppers spill into the streets of Portland, many adorned with Santa hats, elf hats, flashing eye glasses, and other innovative accents—don't forget the glowing ice cubes for their beverages—that would make Clark Griswold jealous.

Participating downtown stores stay open until 10 p.m., often refreshing glasses with free refills (tequila shots, anyone?) in stores along the way. Sales, street performers, carolers, free samples, and giddy gatherings keep the merriment moving.

Sponsored by Portland's Downtown District, this annual tradition is Portland's opportunity to reintroduce the joys of shopping in the city.

Portland Downtown, 549 Congress St., 207-772-6828
portlandmaine.com

THE GIFT OF PORTLAND
AT SPRINGER'S JEWELERS

Iconic landmarks have been treasured holiday gifts in downtown Portland since 1988.

New designs are created every year for the family-run Springer's Jewelers and fabricated into a three-dimensional eighteen-karat-gold-plated brass ornament. Made in the USA, these collectible keepsakes are an annual tradition for locals celebrating Christmastime in their city, snowbirds missing home, or visitors looking to mark the year with a memorable talisman.

"Casco Bay Lines ferry (2006) is our most popular, by far," says Springer's longtime employee Kathi Adams. "The initial order for a thousand was all gone before Christmas! We had to scramble to get more in on time. People love it."

Multi-dimensional ornaments successfully represent the chosen subject. In recent years, splashes of color were added to surprise, including the splash of colored seating in Merrill Auditorium (2017), distinctive red siding and colorful signage of Harbor Fish Market (2016), and green grass at Hadlock Field (2008).

580 Congress St., 800-725-5404
springersjewelers.com

TIP
As the annual ornaments enter their third decade, Portland City Hall (1994) is the first to be retired and no longer available. Alert eBay!

SPARKLE WEEKEND
ON AMTRAK DOWNEASTER'S
SPARKLE EXPRESS

For an old-school way to shop during the holiday season, step aboard the Amtrak Downeaster for a bit of nostalgic elegance. Board at the Portland Transportation Center and travel fifteen miles north. This quick trip brings eager holiday shoppers to Freeport—imagine Fifth Avenue in a Norman Rockwell-style village. Whether the plan is to shop or simply indulge in the festive village's yester-year activities, the town will bring out your inner Christmas Story.

A parade down Main Street of illuminated floats are in keeping with the weekend's theme. Santa leads the crowd to L.L.Bean's world headquarters campus, not coincidentally enveloped by the company's flagship stores. Thousands of lights are choreographed to music for the town's Northern Lights Celebration. The weekend continues with horse-drawn carriage rides, a tuba Christmas concert, and a reindeer petting zoo while children wait to confer with Santa.

Because of Freeport's strict zoning, the walkable town looks like a quiet New England village belying stores like Coach, North Face, Burberry, Oakley, Ralph Lauren Polo, Abercrombie & Fitch, etc. Even the downtown McDonald's is in a country farmhouse—not made to look like one, a real one! When the sales start, they practically pay you to shop!

Portland Transportation Center, 100 Thompson's Point Rd.
800-872-7245, amtrakdowneaster.com/black-friday-fares
Town of Freeport, freeportusa.com

● ●

SHOP FARM-TO-TABLE
AT OLDEST U.S. FARMERS MARKET

Every Saturday morning, spring through late fall, foodies and gardeners descend on Deering Oaks Park. They shop for the freshest ingredients, flowers, plants, and crafts Maine has to offer...that week. Every Wednesday, a similar ritual of commerce occurs amid the high rises of Monument Square. In the cold-weather months, the market moves to an indoor location in the Deering neighborhood. For two-and-a-half centuries, Portland's farmers market has continuously been bringing fresh farm produce, meat, plants, and crafts to its urban center and many of the best restaurants. Being part of that tradition is a bit humbling.

Shortly before the revolution in 1768, Portland—then known as Falmouth—established a public market in the town hall to regulate the food being sold by rural farmers. After the revolution, the city (renamed Portland) made Market Square (now Monument Square) home to the Farmers Market. Consistently rated one of the top markets in the U.S., it's almost as important socially as it is commercially. Family and friends schedule their days around it, some making it a weekly gathering.

Deering Oaks Park, Saturdays 7 a.m. to 1 p.m., May-November
Maine Girls' Academy, 631 Stevens Ave., Saturdays 9 a.m. to 1 p.m.,
December-April
Monument Square, Wednesdays 7 a.m. to 1 p.m., year 'round
portlandmainefarmersmarket.org

CHARMING PORTLAND
WITH CH*ART* METALWORKS

"Casco Bay is the most popular design with out-of-state customers—it encompasses the largest area of Portland," says Charlotte Guptill of her jewelry line's navigation-chart accents. CHART Metalworks exploded on the scene in 2006 when avid sailor Guptill, after abandoning a career as a loan officer, began to incorporate snippets of nautical maps into pendants being created in her fledgling business. The in-demand Casco Bay collection features pewter and sterling silver pieces cast in Maine, accented with adornments of tiny charts highlighting Portland's waterfront. Charts depict the downtown peninsula with Back Bay, Casco Bay, and the Calendar Islands, as well as a map of the entire state. Drawing inspiration from their boating theme, CHART Metalworks recently introduced bronze. Known by sailors to never rust or tarnish, the metal forms a lovely patina over time.

The jewelry line now includes earrings, bracelets, and accessories—even cufflinks and other menswear. "Our biggest sellers are key rings," smiles Guptill. "They're one size fits all, and appeal to young and old, men and women."

From their studio overlooking a statue of Portland native John Ford, custom orders nationwide have evolved to include inland maps. Like the famous director outside, Guptill knows how to convey a map of the human heart.

1 Pleasant St., 207-221-6807
chartmetalworks.com

130

HAVE A BROMANCE
AT MENSROOM

Men often dumbfounded at the cost of women's hairstyling will be perplexed no more—or at least have a deeper appreciation after this guilty pleasure in the Mensroom. The innovative man-cave salon can make even the most Alpha Male betray his $10-haircut barber. Tuesday's two-for-one haircut and style may also have them redefine date night as well, when bringing a buddy cuts the price in half.

Entering the exposed-brick shop, long-haired patrons are greeted by a smiling hostess who offers complimentary coffee, wine, or beer. A window-side table overlooks Monument Square while a leather couch and recliners surround a large flat-screen, often televising news or sports. A dart board and pool table offer active distractions while waiting for an appointment.

When it's time, stylists lead their clientele away to plush chairs, beginning by sloughing off stress with a shoulder and head massage. The relaxation continues as a heated towel envelopes the face with selected scents while hair is washed and conditioned. Artistically styled, the final touches leave customers feeling fresh, and fully rejuvenated.

If not, there's always time for another game of Eight Ball and a beer.

8 City Center, 207-874-8080
mensroomsalon.com

COME SAIL AWAY
AT SEA BAGS

"All our bags are made from recycled sails," says Sea Bags employee Justin Holdefer about the fashion-forward tote. "If you bring in a sail, we'll make your bag for free based on its size."

The Custom House Wharf company's innovative twist on the working waterfront encourages customers to design bags to fit their personality. Each item is hand-stitched to ensure quality and uniqueness—"each bag is truly one of a kind." Bags are brandished as fashion statements and spotted by locals miles away.

Sails are also turned into various sized bags, luggage tags, and wine totes. For customers who'd rather stick with traditional designs, "The Navy Anchor design is our most popular tote right now," says Holdefer. "The Octopus Tote lined with Charles Darwin's notes is also a big seller."

24 Custom House Wharf, 207-780-0744

seabags.com

KEEP IT SIMPLE
WITH JILL McGOWAN

"I started...with two guiding principles: to create beautiful clothing that is comfortable and fashionable, and to make clothing of quality that will endure fashion changes and wear well," says Jill McGowan. Launched in 1994, her elegant all-cotton white shirts' clean lines and durable craftsmanship resonated with women, uncovering an unexpectedly high-end niché. McGowan's "Great White Shirt" designs quickly garnered attention from fashion magazines and other media, including a heralded visit from Martha Stewart. Her in-town studio was flooded with orders from retailers nationwide. Jill McGowan clothing is now sold nationwide and makes cameo appearances on television and in films. But the native Mainer still calls Portland home.

McGowan has since deviated from simple white blouses, but stays true to her vision. Still American made, fabrics include knits and blends. Designs also venture into patterns, textures, and even a color palette. Other garments make bolder statements, trading the traditional white for strong red, blue, or black solids. McGowan's casual line, 94 Portland, is more adventurous with whimsical patterns playing off an even broader spectrum of color. But don't be fooled—white is still the new black.

Studio: 45 Casco St., 207-772-2199
jillmcgowan.com

Flagship store: 56 Main St., Freeport, 207-865-0909

• •

THE SUITE LIFE
AT THE PRESS HOTEL

While many hotels in Portland offer opulent accommodations, The Press Hotel's penthouse suite is unlike any other. Room 701 sits atop the Gannett Building, former home of the *Portland Press Herald* newspaper. Complete with fireplace, open kitchen/dining room, and spacious living room, this luxurious 1,110-square-foot one-bedroom suite's greatest attribute is the outdoor rooftop deck with expansive views of the city and harbor. Clever nods to its newsprint heyday are sprinkled about, most notably chairs emblazoned with the phrase familiar to every journalism student—"The quick brown fox jumped over the lazy dog."

In fact, the 1923 city-block-big brick edifice was at one time not only home to the paper's newsrooms, but the printing press as well—all completely transformed into a luxury boutique hotel.

But this clever adaptive reuse did not ignore the paper's storied past, it embraced it! A vintage typewriter art installation spirals in organized chaos over the lobby's central stairway. The former City Room serves as the lobby, capped with The Inkwell lounge. Homages to the letterpress days are found throughout the inn. The front entrance windows are comprised of letterpress trays while the front desk, signage, and various accents also evoke the lost industraial art form. Even the carpet's pattern realistically emulates type blocks spilling across the hallways while walls are decorated with actual headlines from decades past.

119 Exchange St., 207-808-8800

thepresshotel.com

● ●

The Gannett Building
(a.k.a. *Portland Press Herald* Building)

Built in 1923

Tapestry brick and stone building across from
city hall (with decommissioned underground
tunnel connecting the buildings)

Adjoining building added in 1947

*Portland Press Herald & Maine Sunday
Telegram* moved operations in 2010 to
One Monument Square

Developer Jim Brady opens
The Press Hotel in 2015

110-room boutique luxury hotel, part the
Autograph Collection Hotels

Woven wall tapestries
by local designer Angela Adams

Fun Fact: Scale used for weighing
the huge rolls of newsprint restored and
relocated in the fitness center

SUGGESTED
ITINERARIES

COUPLES

CREATIVES

FAMILIES

HISTORIANS

ADVENTURERS & EXPLORERS

FOODIES

URBANITES

QUIET SEEKERS

SPENDTHRIFTS & WINDOW SHOPPERS

NIGHT OWLS

AUTHENTIC MAINE

ACTIVITIES
BY SEASON

WINTER

SPRING

• •

SUMMER

FALL

• •

INDEX